I0465572

©

All rights reserved

Cristian Romero Vargas

To my father Pedro Romero, who gave me the gift of music and by his example has taught me that it is always possible to improve. Thank you!

INTRODUCTION

This book is born from the need to fill a gap in the intervalic and harmonic education offered to string musicians. Violin has a literature of etudes and methods designed to cover all the technical aspects of the instrument so extensively that in fact it is almost impossible to seriously approach and work each and every one of them during the formative period.

There are hundreds of etudes for working bow strokes (detaché, martelé, spicatto, stacato, legato...) and for the left hand (changes of position, extensions, double strings, pizzicato, harmonics...) of so recognized pedagogues as Kreutzer, Sevcik, Dont, Schradieck, Rodé among others, that in fact the great problem of pedagogues, teachers and the study methods, is often the selection of criteria when choosing or discarding certain methodology for the student, who, besides the practice of etudes and scales, he must practice one or several repertoire pieces.

However, despite the large number of methods for violin, there is still a gap in the intervalic and harmonic work for this instrument. A method that gradually and progressively can address these aspects that have been worked a lot more for other instruments such as the piano or guitar, but not as extensively for the violin.

With this book you will learn how to play, understand, and connect all the major, minor, diminished, and augmented triads. Every measure is design so when you play it, you can understand how it fits in its corresponding chord, whether it is in root position, first inversion or second inversion.

HOW TO STUDY THIS BOOK?

I recommend working first playing each studio a couple of times or three times, until the sonority is in our ear and we have the melodic drawing in our head. After this, we must analyze the study and look at how it is built, how it links and where it goes.

Once we have understood how it is built, we must try to build it ourselves without the score, this is the end of the studies, to encourage conscious and reflective study. WE MUST NOT LEARN THEM BY MEMORY, we must understand them and know how to build them on the fly.

PRACTICE ORDER

Although the studies are listed from 1 to 48, it is recommended that they be studied first the major triads, then the minor triads, diminished triads, and finally the augmented triads.

Working with this method you will achieve great technical freedom because these new studies prepare the modern violinist for the current violin repertoire, improving the sight reading and accelerating the learning of new repertoires, as well as serving for a better understanding of the fingerboard and significantly improve the intonation.

INTRODUCCIÓN

Nace este libro de la necesidad de cubrir un vacío en la educación interválica y armónica que se brinda a los músicos de cuerda. Tiene el Violín una literatura de estudios y métodos destinados a cubrir todos los aspectos técnicos del instrumento tan extensa y amplia que de hecho es casi imposible abordar y trabajar de manera responsable todos y cada uno de ellos durante el periodo de formación.

Hay cientos de estudios para trabajar golpes de arco (detaché, martelé, spicatto, estacato, ligadas...) y para la mano izquierda (cambios de posición, extensiones, dobles cuerdas, pizzicato, armónicos...) de pedagogos tan reconocidos como Kreutzer, Sevcik, Dont, Schradieck, Rodé entre otros, que de hecho el gran problema de pedagogos, maestros y planes de estudio está muchas veces en el criterio de selección a la hora de escoger o desechar determinados estudios o métodos al estudiante, ya que como es lógico además de la práctica de estudios y escalas debemos practicar una o varias obras.

Sin embargo y pese a la gran cantidad de métodos que hay para violín sigue habiendo un vacío en el trabajo interválico y armónico para este instrumento. Un método que de forma gradual y progresiva aborde estos aspectos un poco más trabajados en otros instrumentos como el piano o la guitarra, que dada su naturaleza se prestan más para ello, pero no por eso deben estos aspectos olvidarse de trabajar en el violín.

Con este libro aprenderá a tocar, reconocer y enlazar todas las tríadas mayores, menores, disminuidas y aumentadas. Todos los compases están cifrados para que a la vez que se tocan se vaya tomando conciencia del acorde, unas veces en estado fundamental y otras en primera o segunda inversión.

¿CÓMO ESTUDIAR ESTE LIBRO?

Recomiendo trabajar primero tocando cada estudio un par de veces o tres, hasta que la sonoridad esté en nuestro oído y tengamos el dibujo melódico en nuestra cabeza. Después de esto, debemos analizar el estudio y mirar cómo está construido, cómo enlaza y hacia donde va.

Una vez hayamos comprendido cómo está construido, debemos intentar construirlo nosotros solos sin la partitura, este es el fin de los estudios, fomentar el estudio consciente y reflexivo. NO DEBEMOS APRENDERLOS DE MEMORIA, debemos entenderlos y saber construirlos sobre la marcha.

ORDEN DE ESTUDIO

A pesar de que los estudios están enumerados del 1 al 48, se recomienda su estudio empezando primero por las tríadas mayores, después las menores, disminuidas y por ultimo las aumentadas.

Trabajando con este método alcanzará una gran libertad técnica pues estos nuevos estudios preparan al violinista moderno para el actual repertorio del violín, mejorando la primera vista y acelerando el aprendizaje de nuevos repertorios, además de servir para una mejor comprensión del diapasón y mejorar sensiblemente la afinación.

Etude 1-3-5
Major and minor

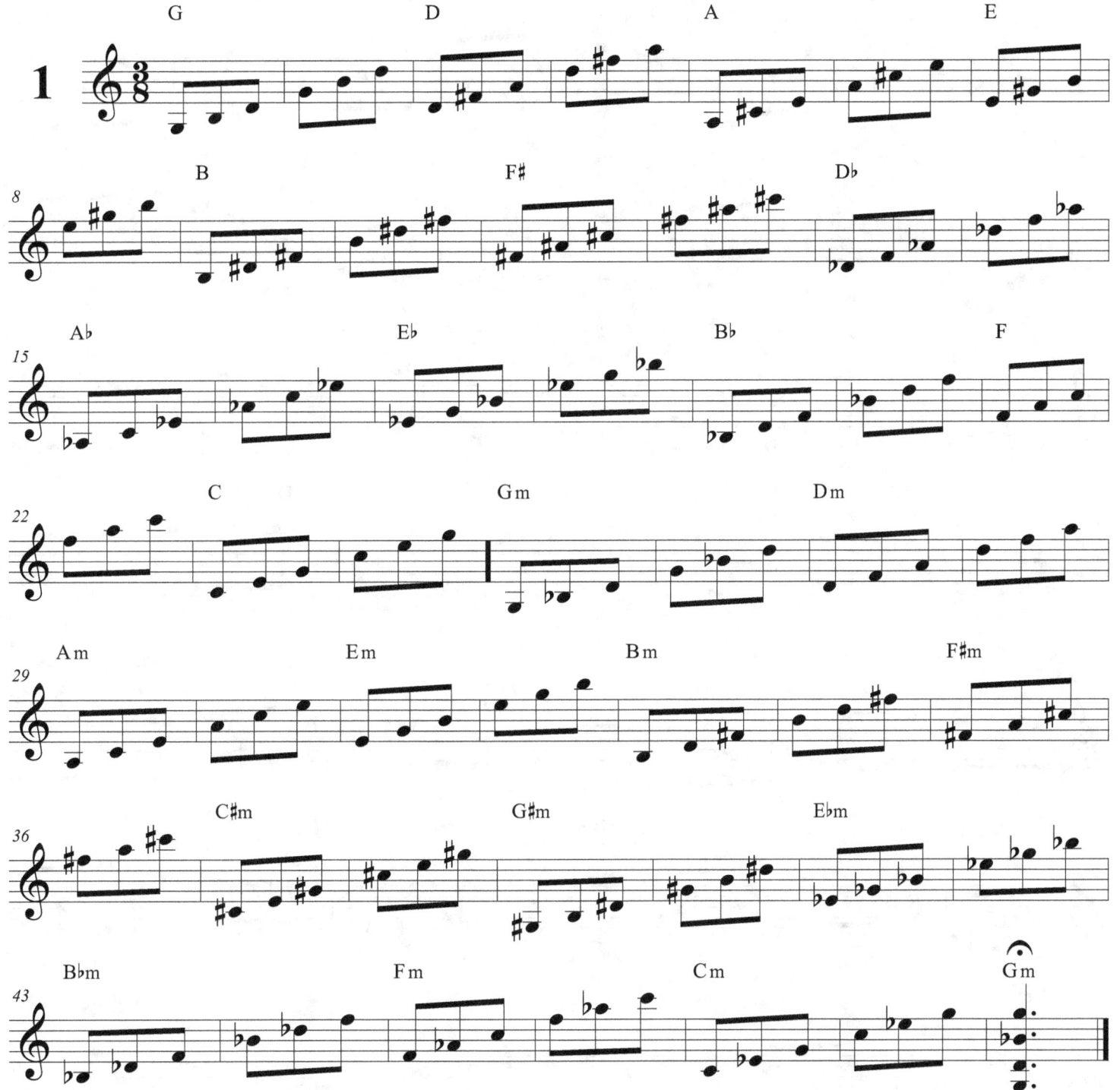

Variation 1-3-5
Major and minor

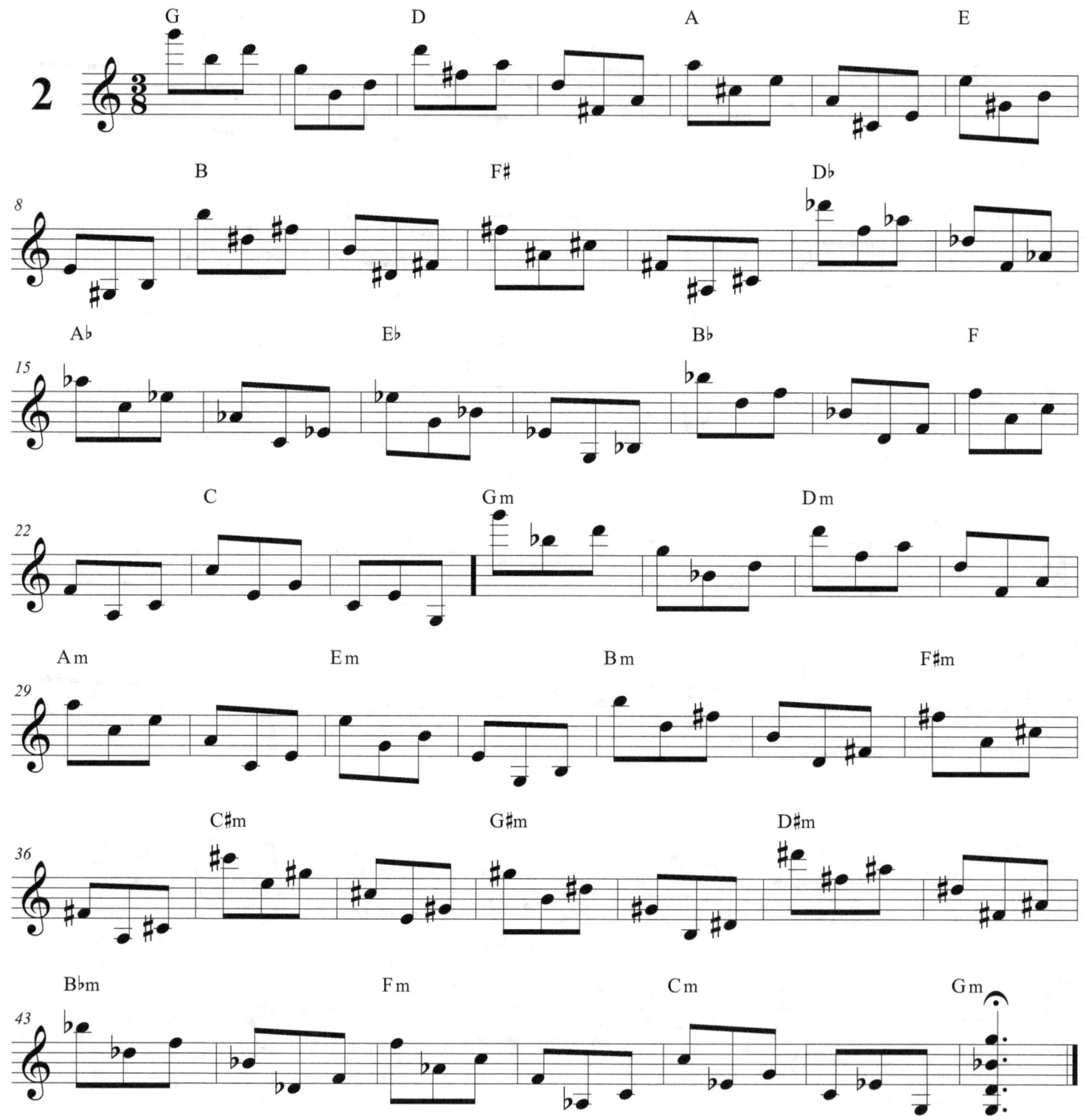

Etude 1-3-5
Diminished and augmented

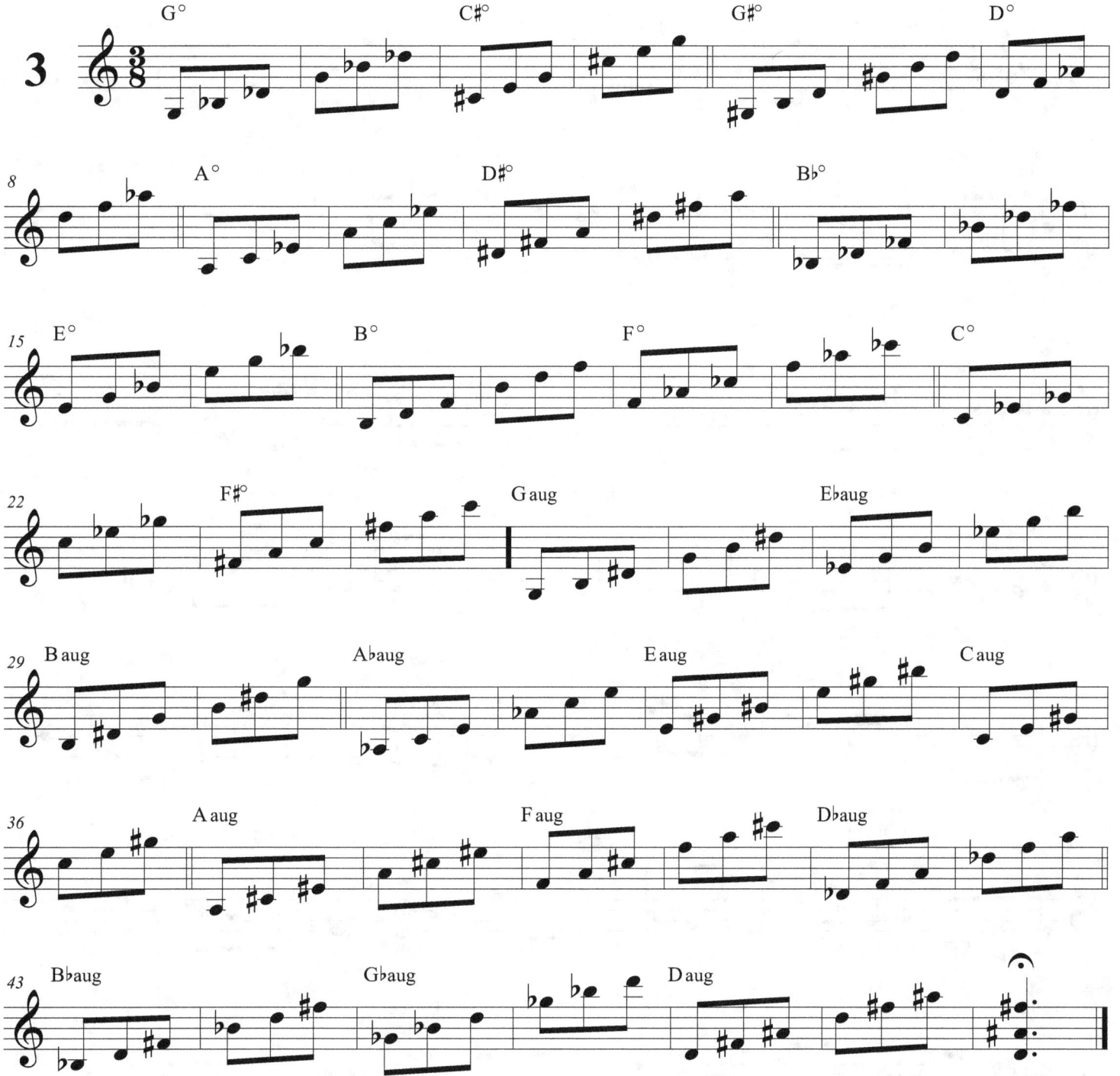

Variation 1-3-5
Diminished and augmented

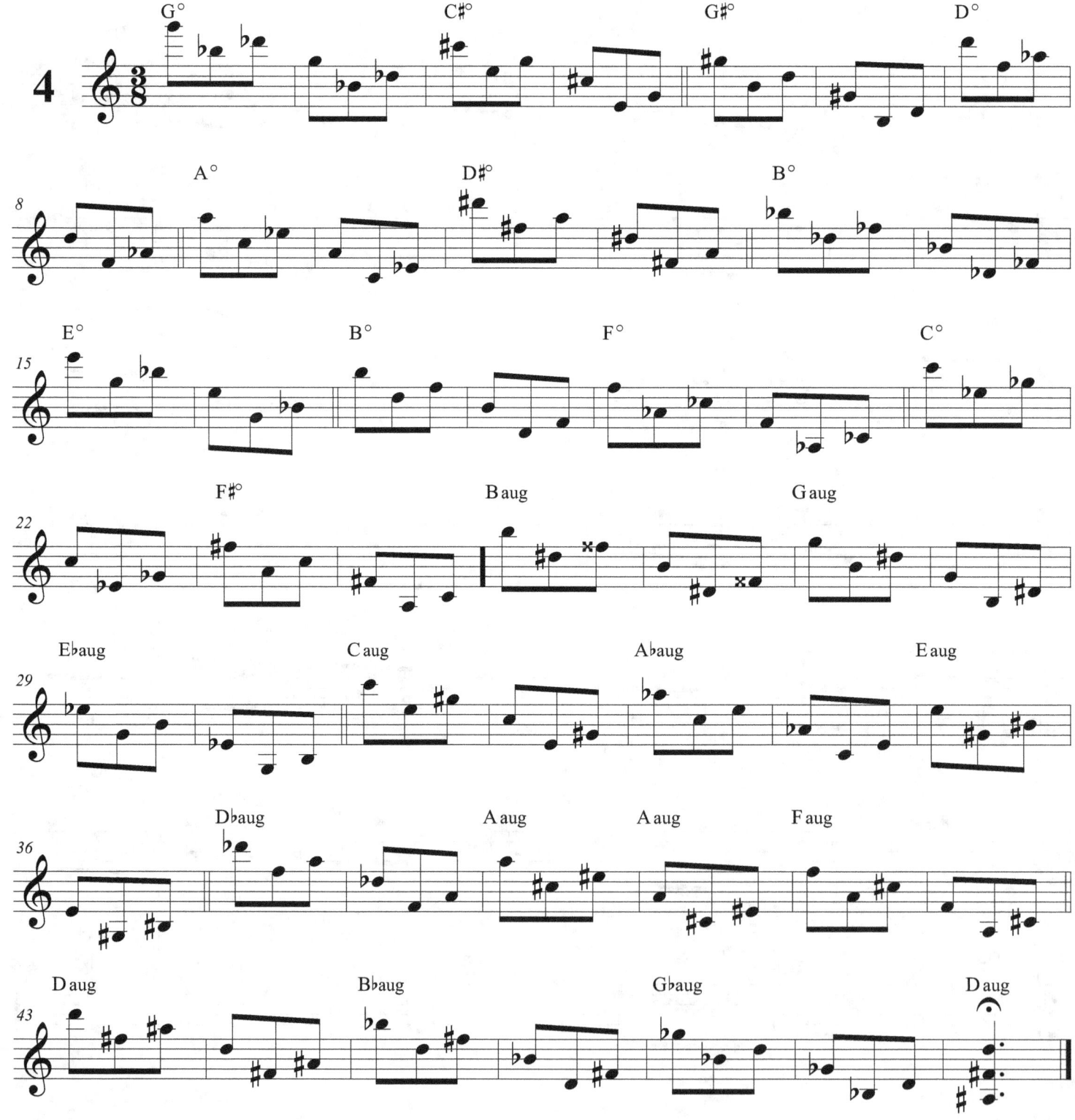

Etude 1-5-3
Major and minor

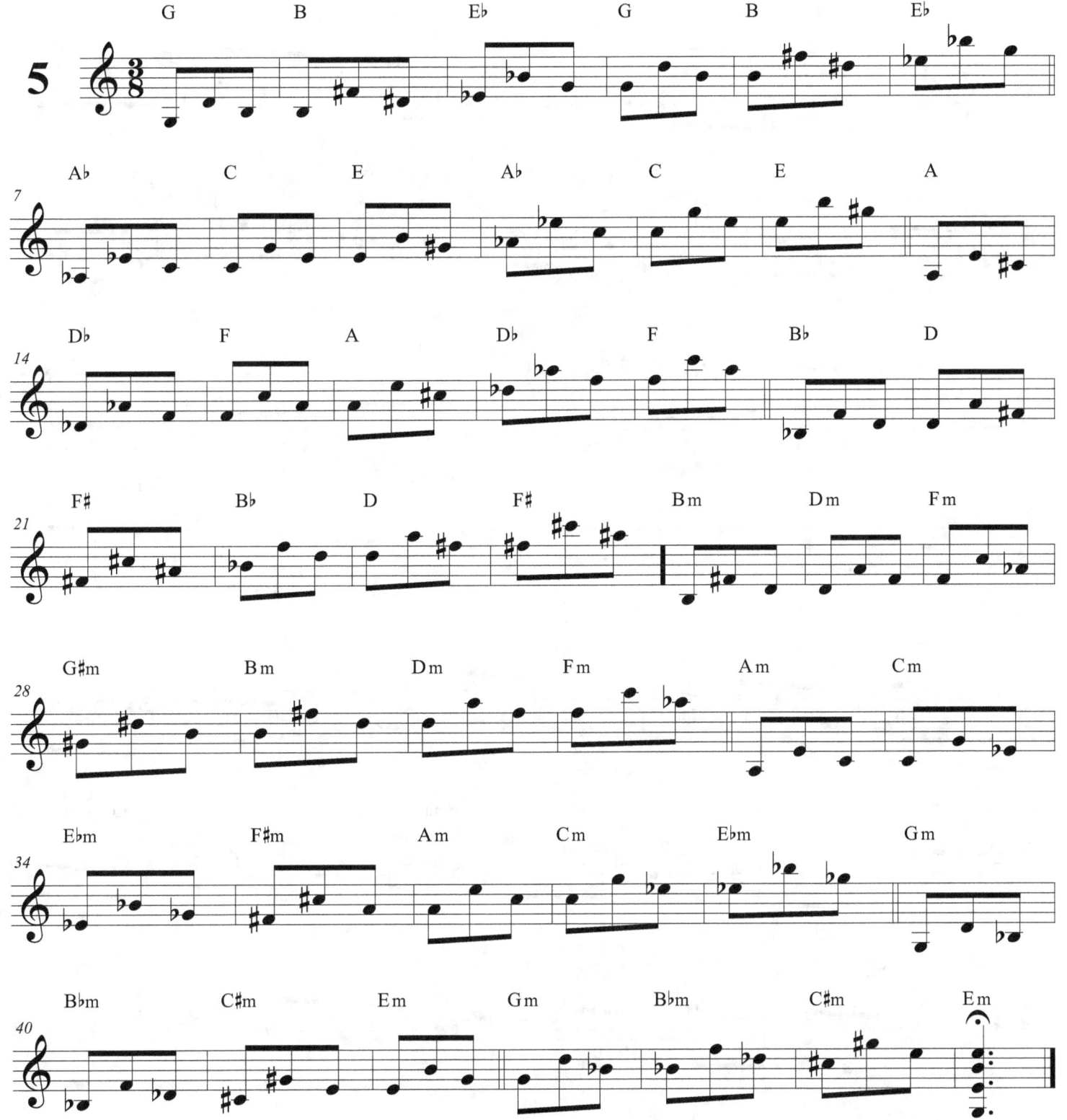

Variation 1-5-3
Major and minor

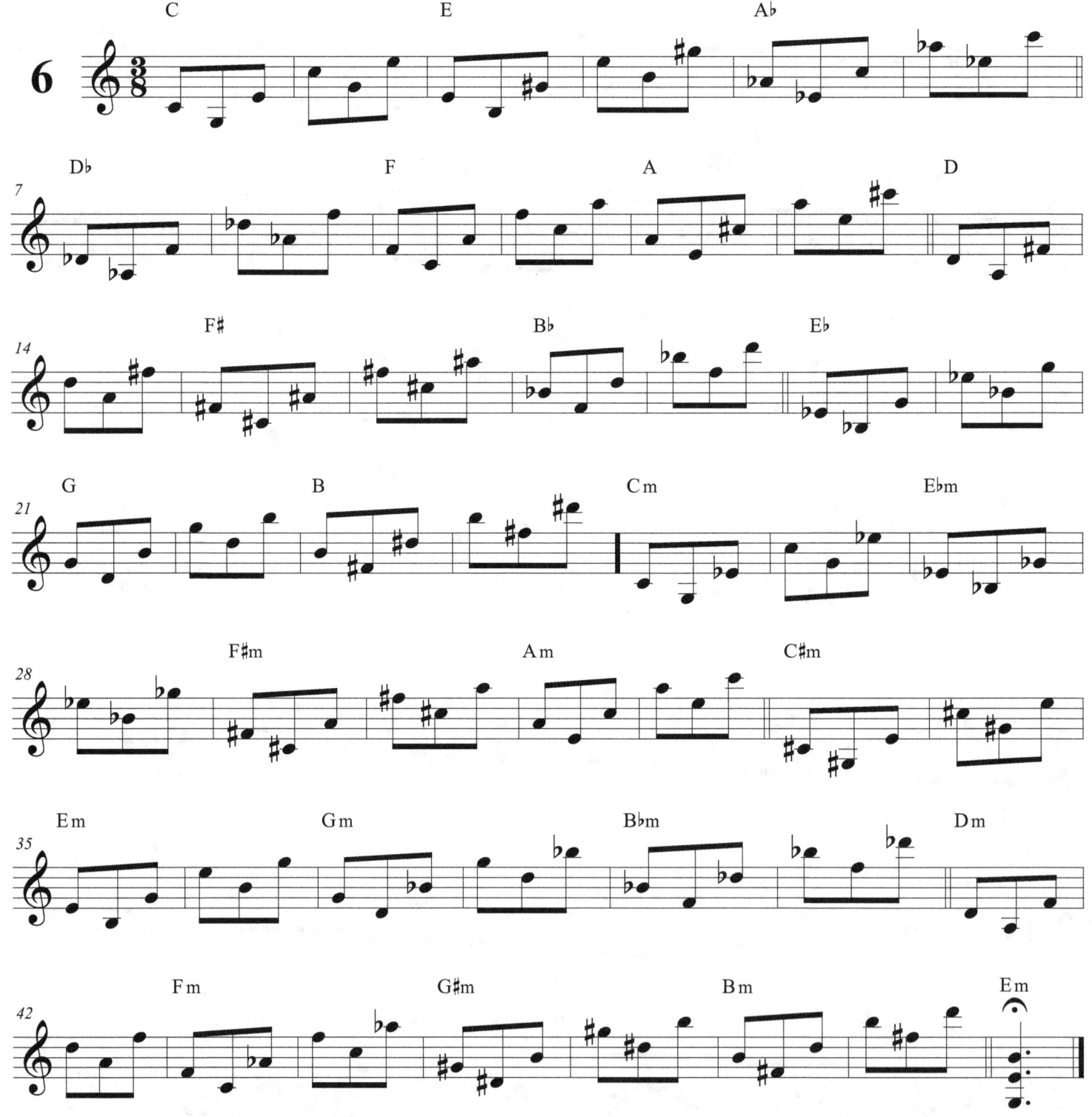

Etude 1-5-3
Diminished and augmented

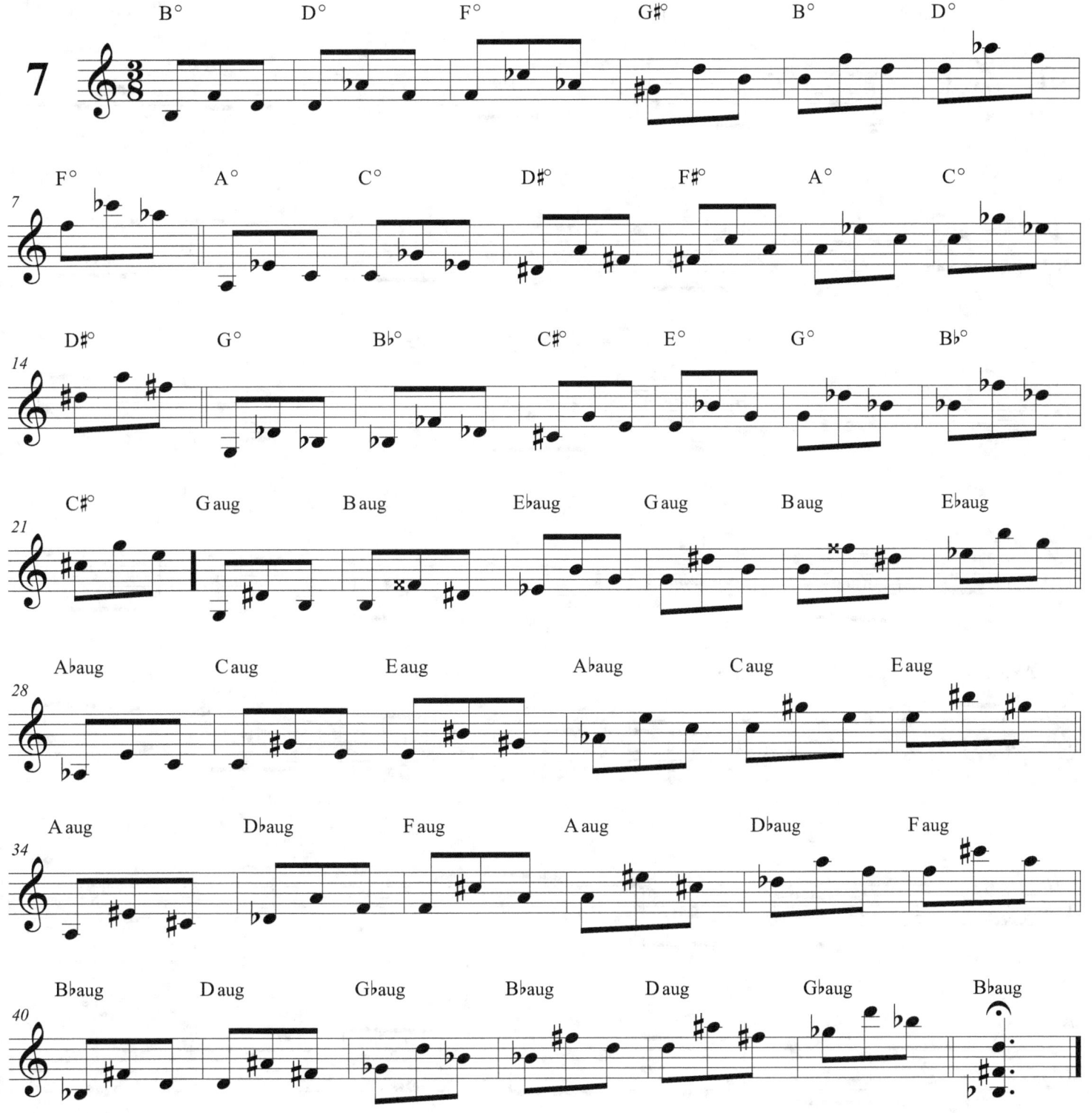

Variation 1-5-3
Diminished y augmented

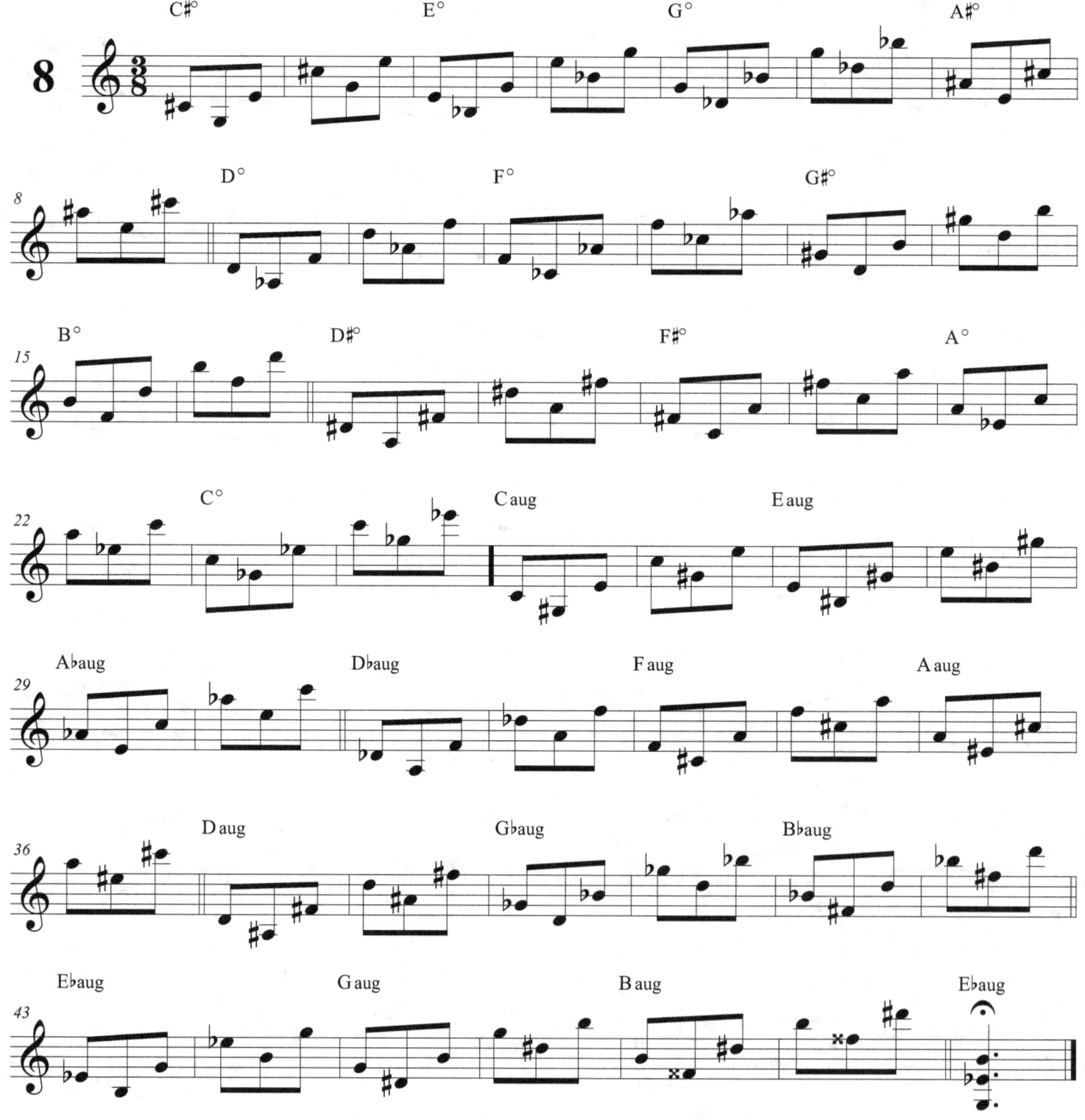

Etude 3-1-5
Major

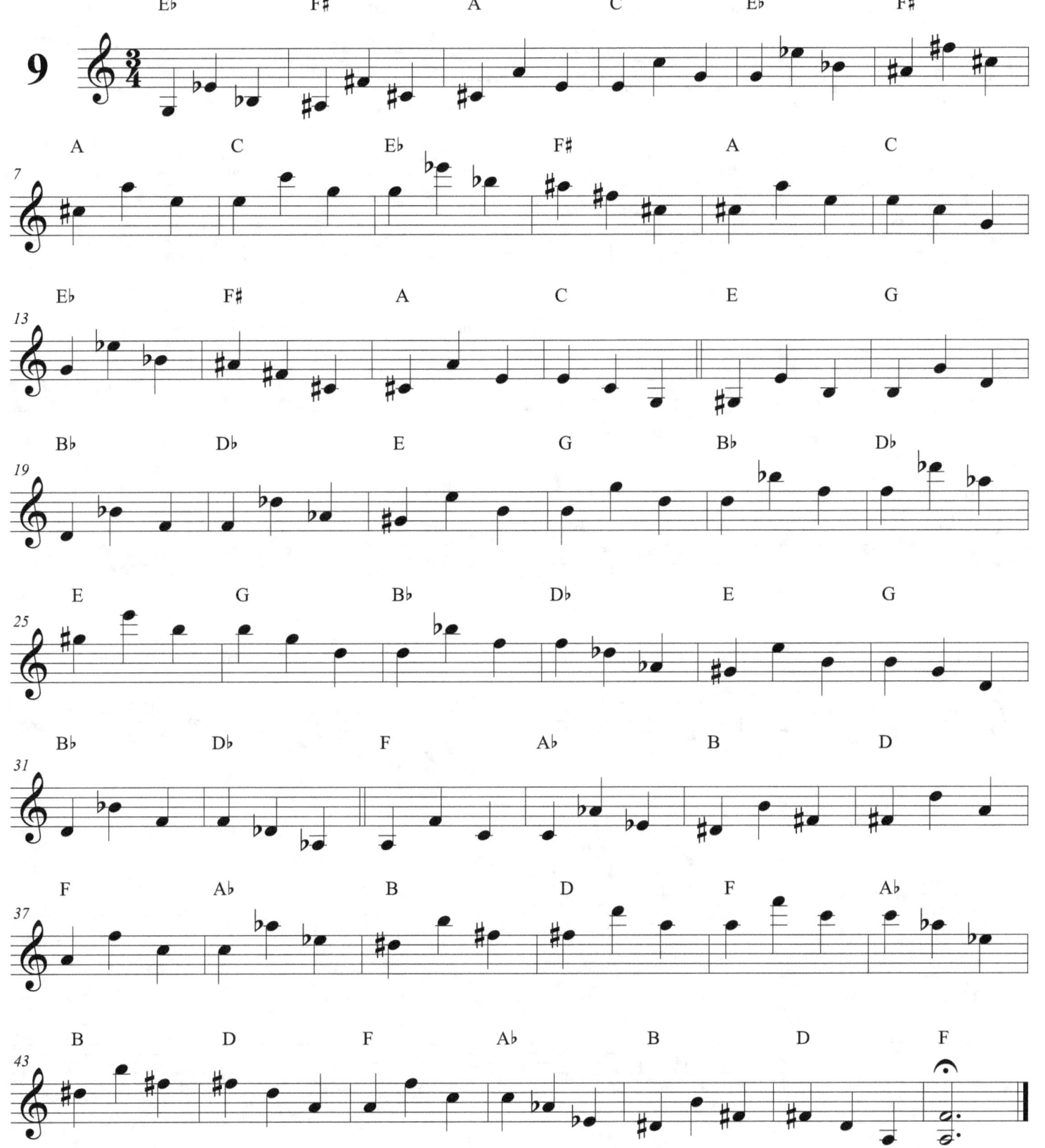

Etude 3-1-5
Minor

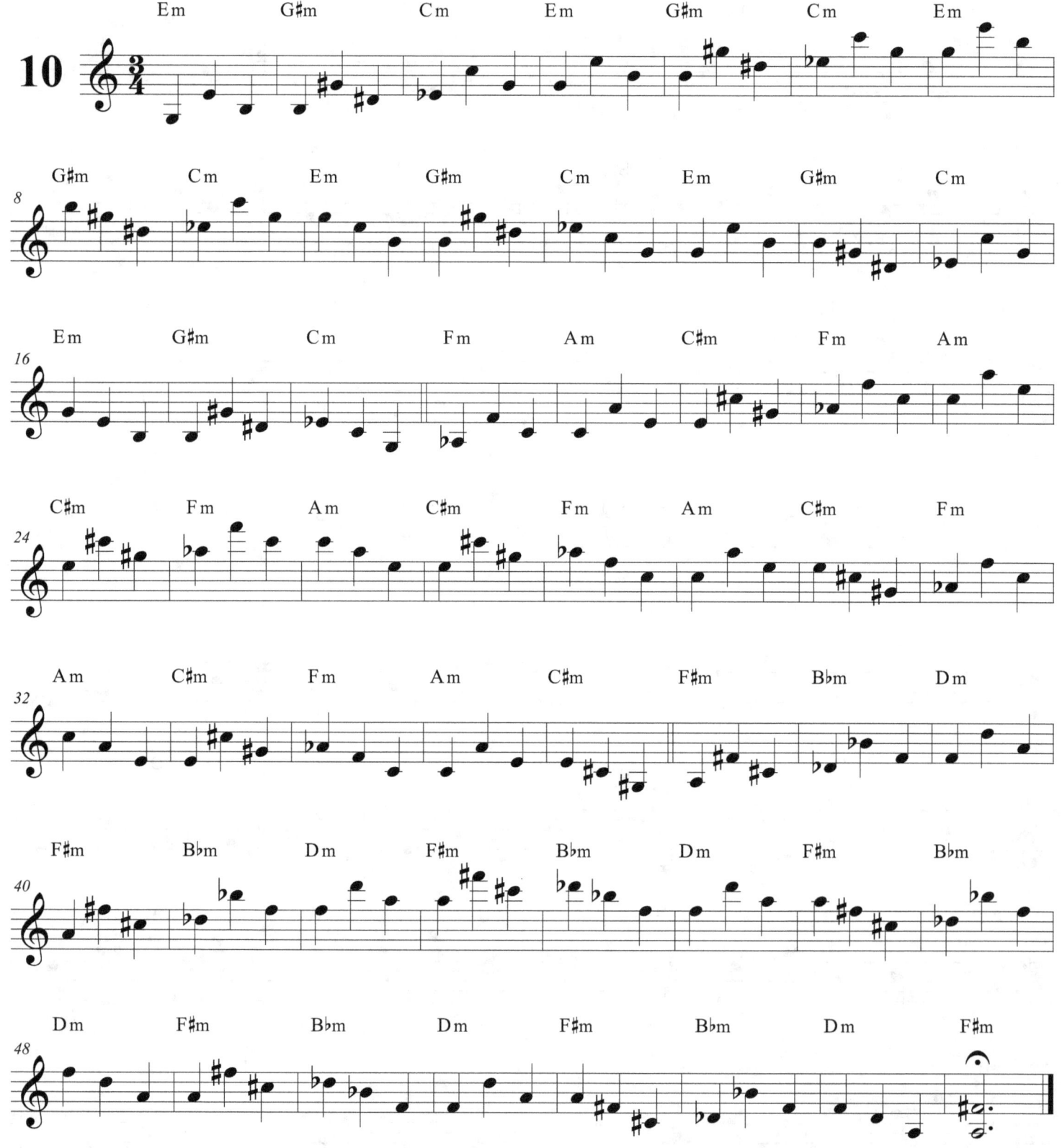

Etude 3-1-5
Diminished

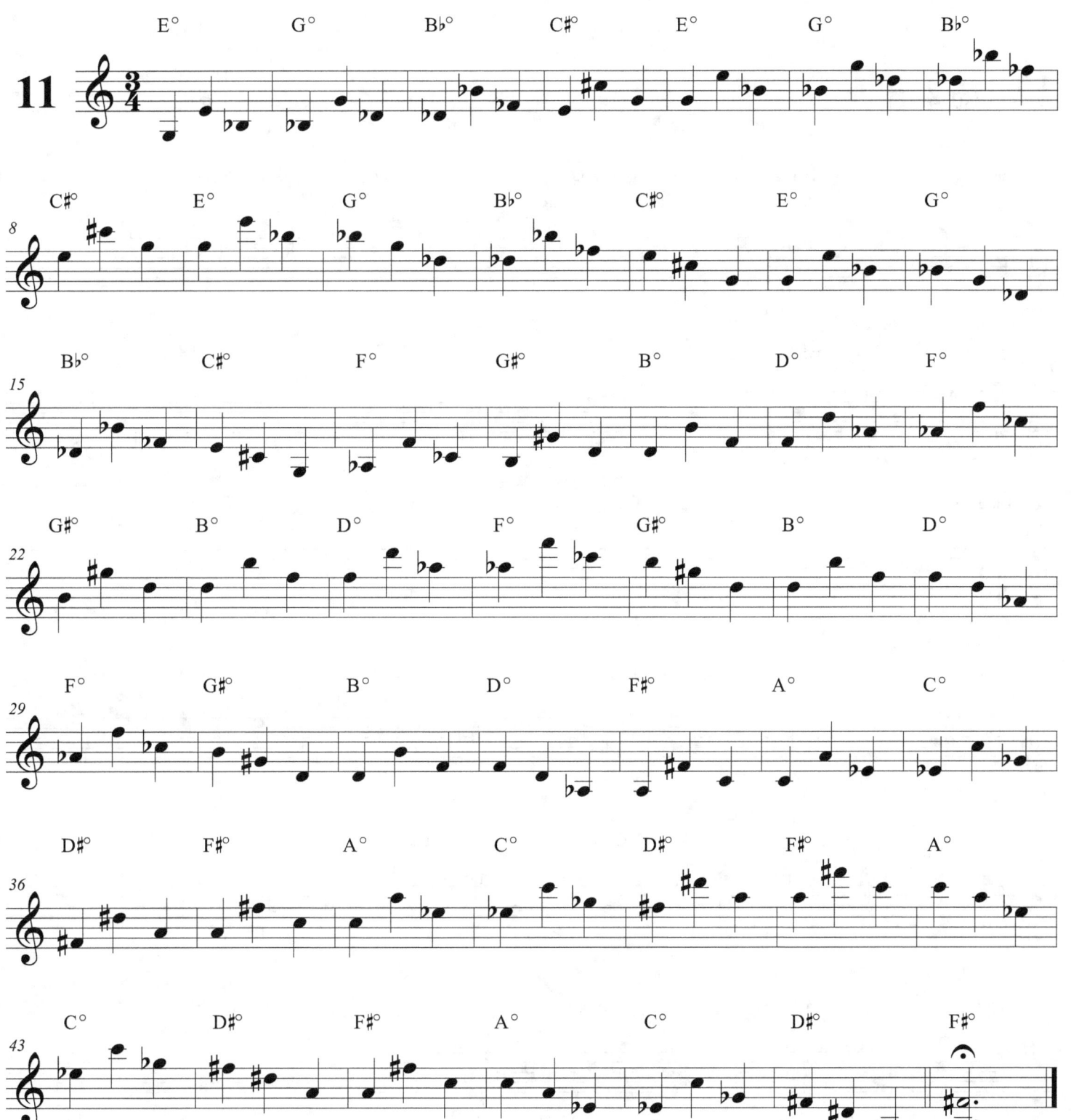

Etude 3-1-5
Augmented

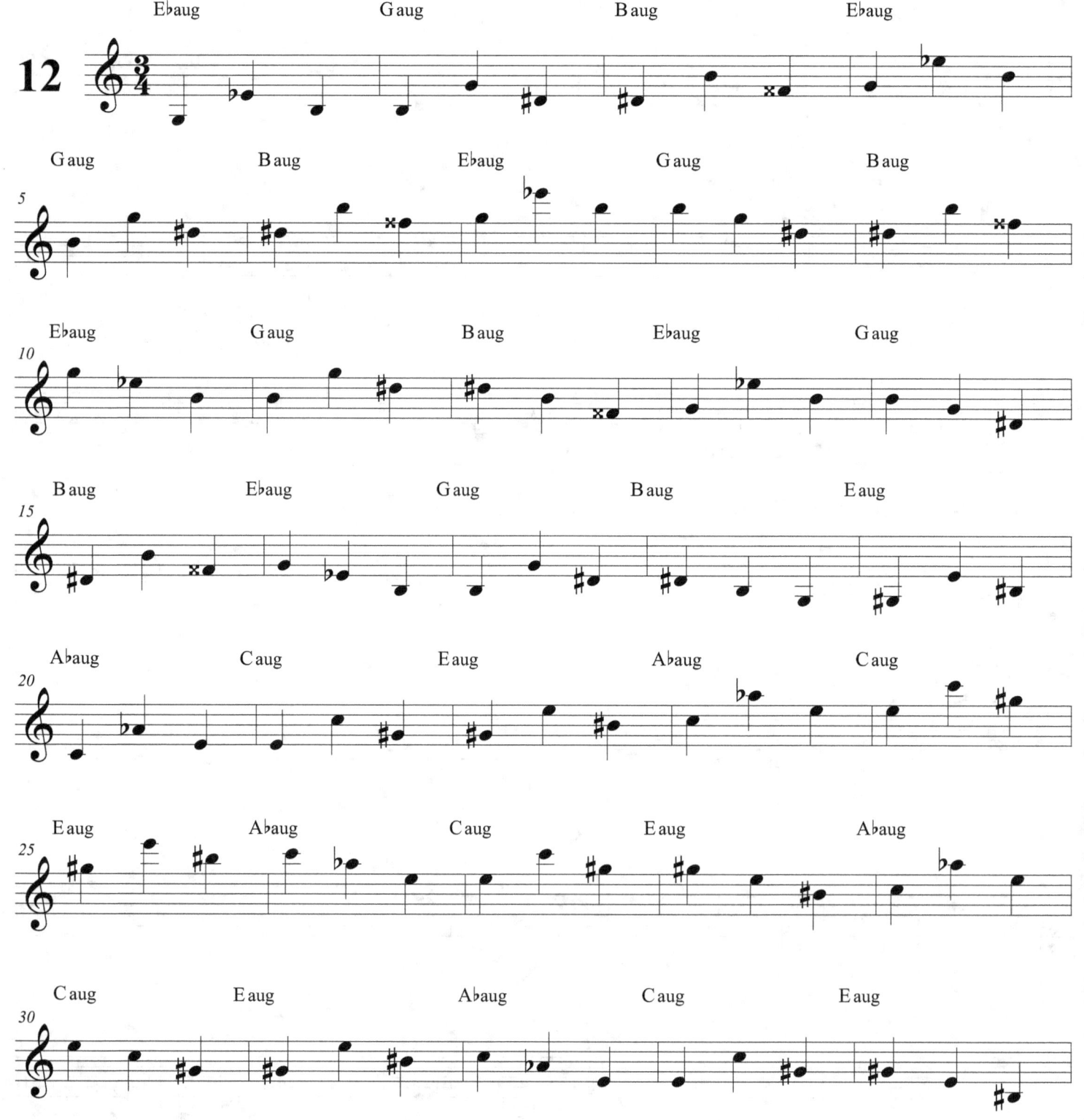

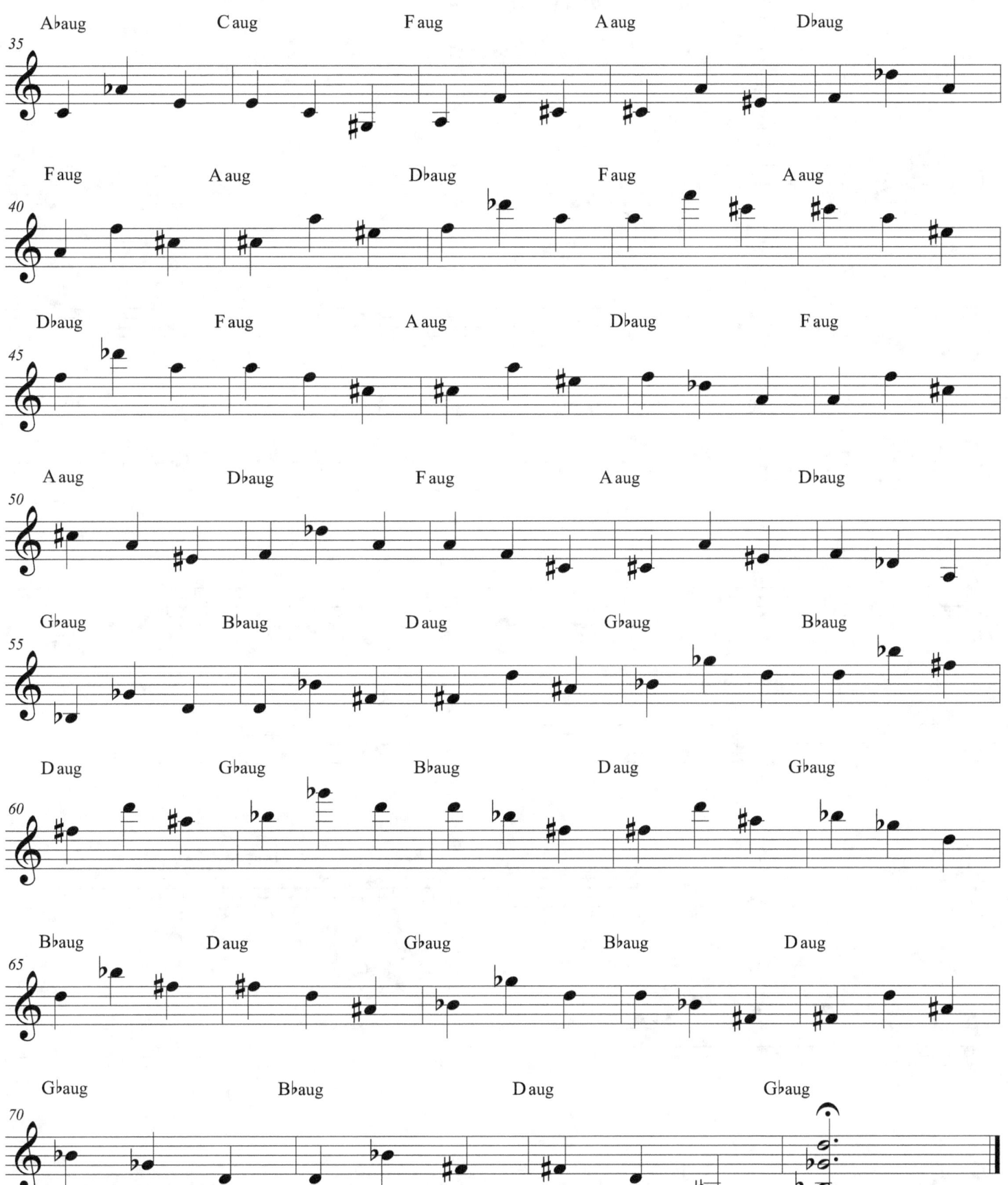

Etude 3-5-1
Major

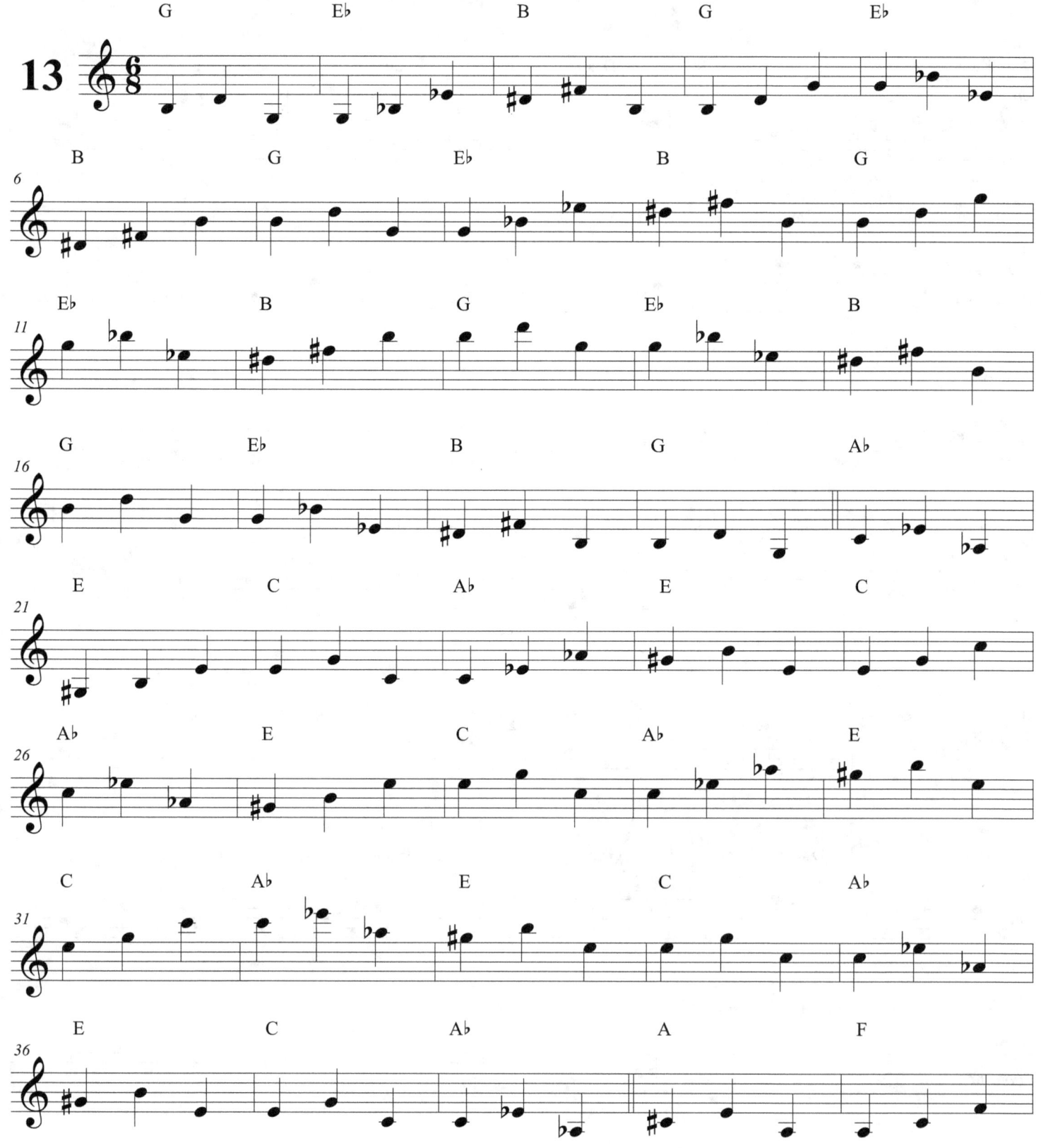

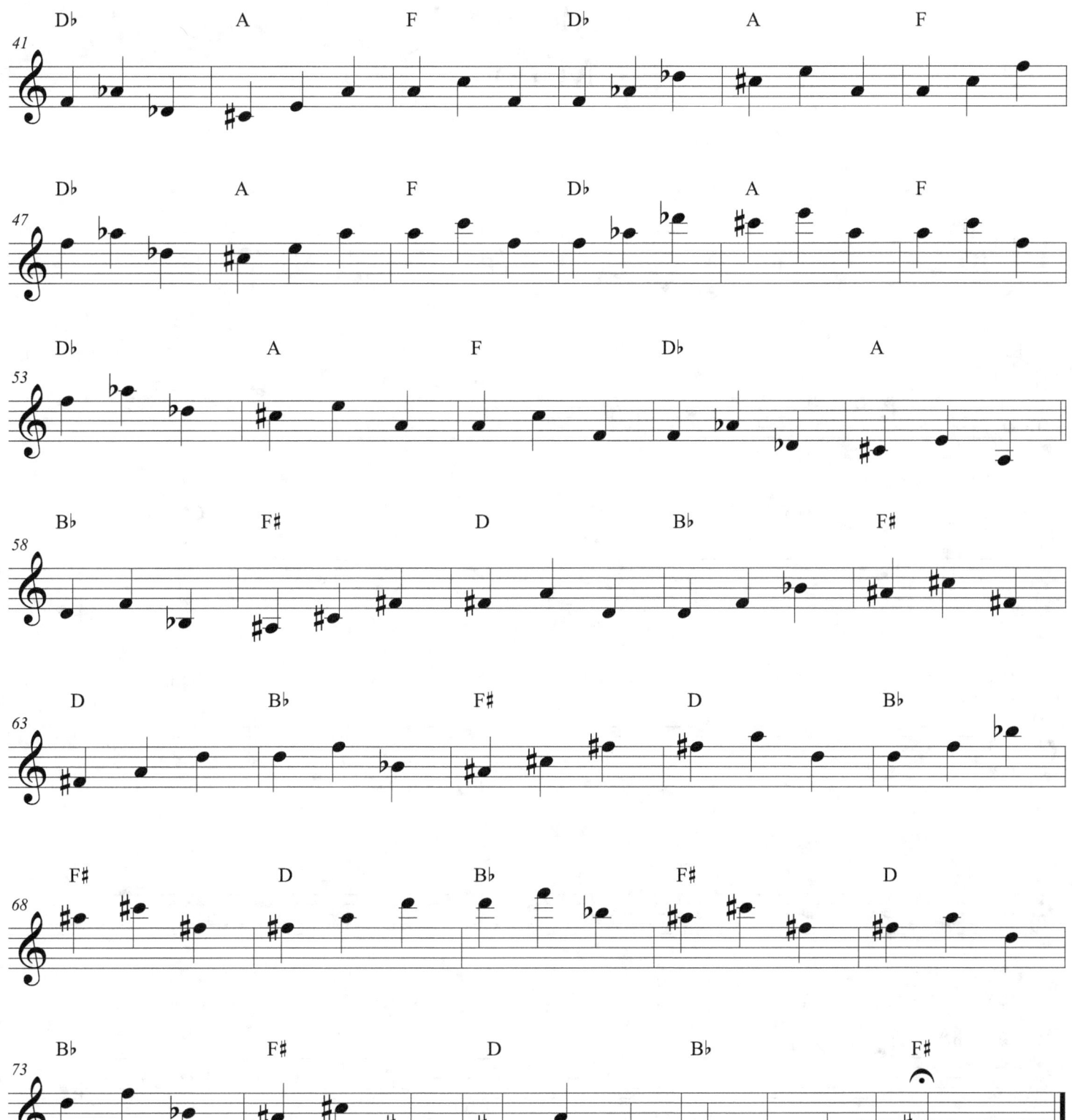

Etude 3-5-1
Minor

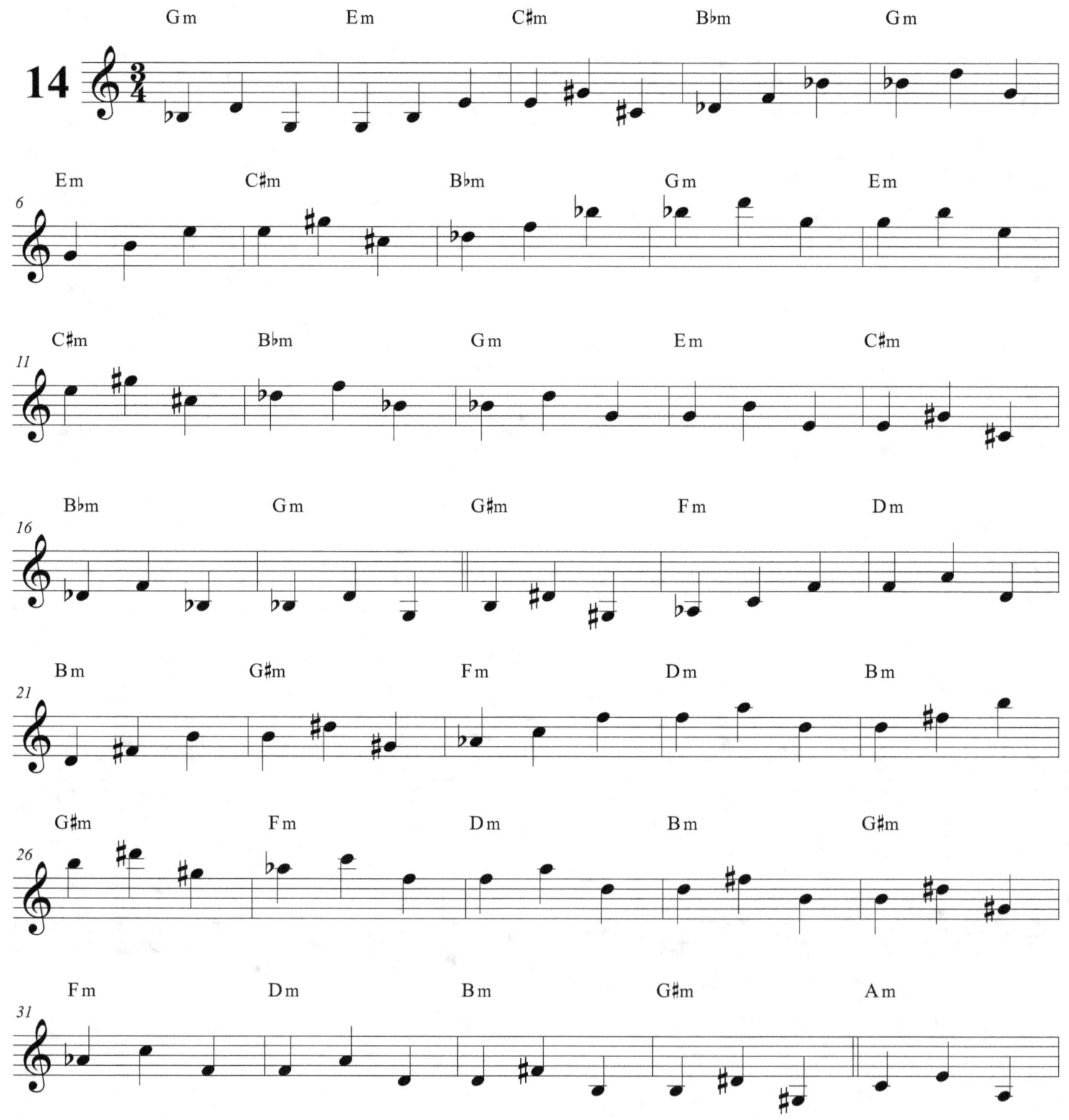

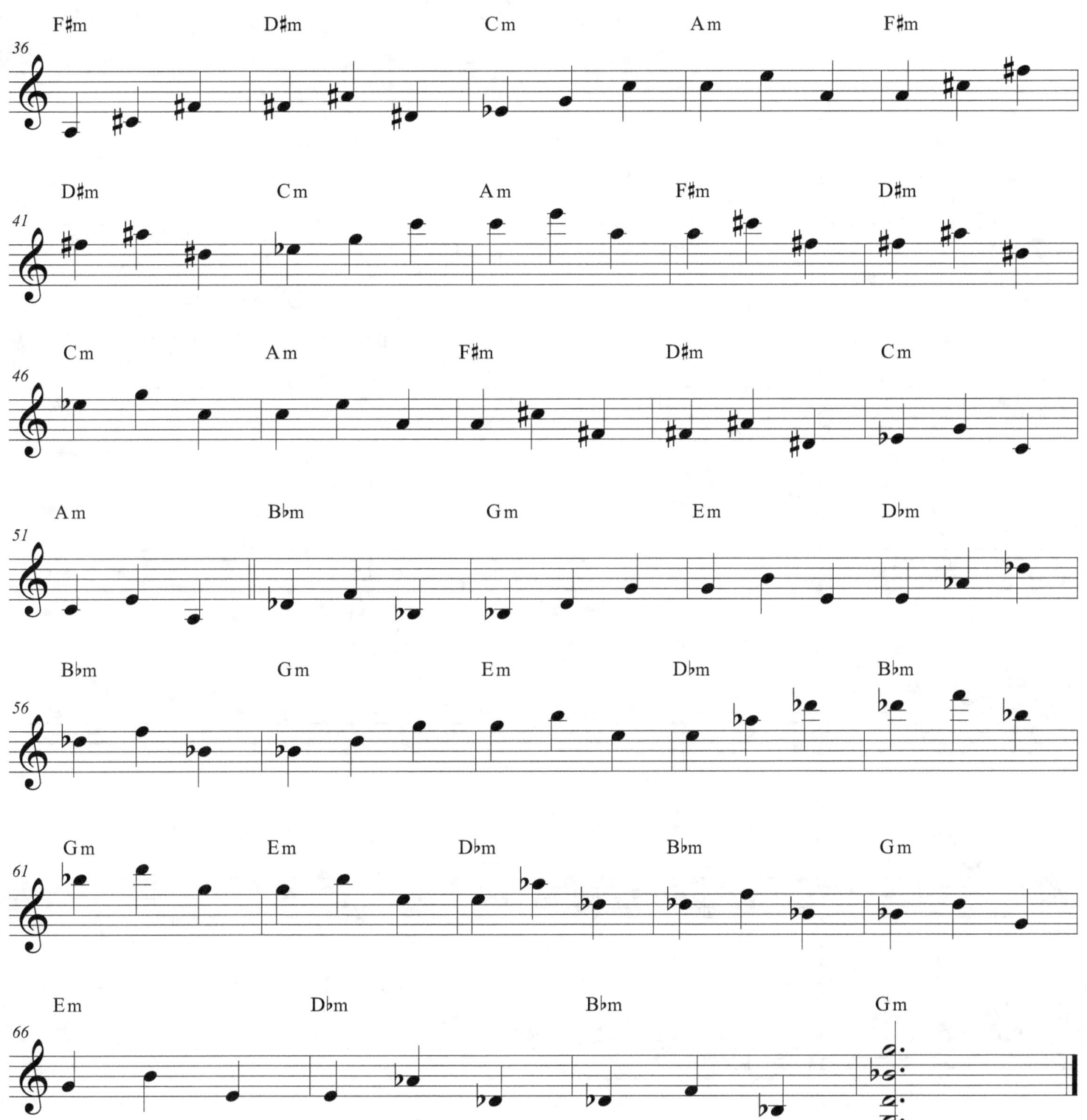

Etude 3-5-1
Diminished

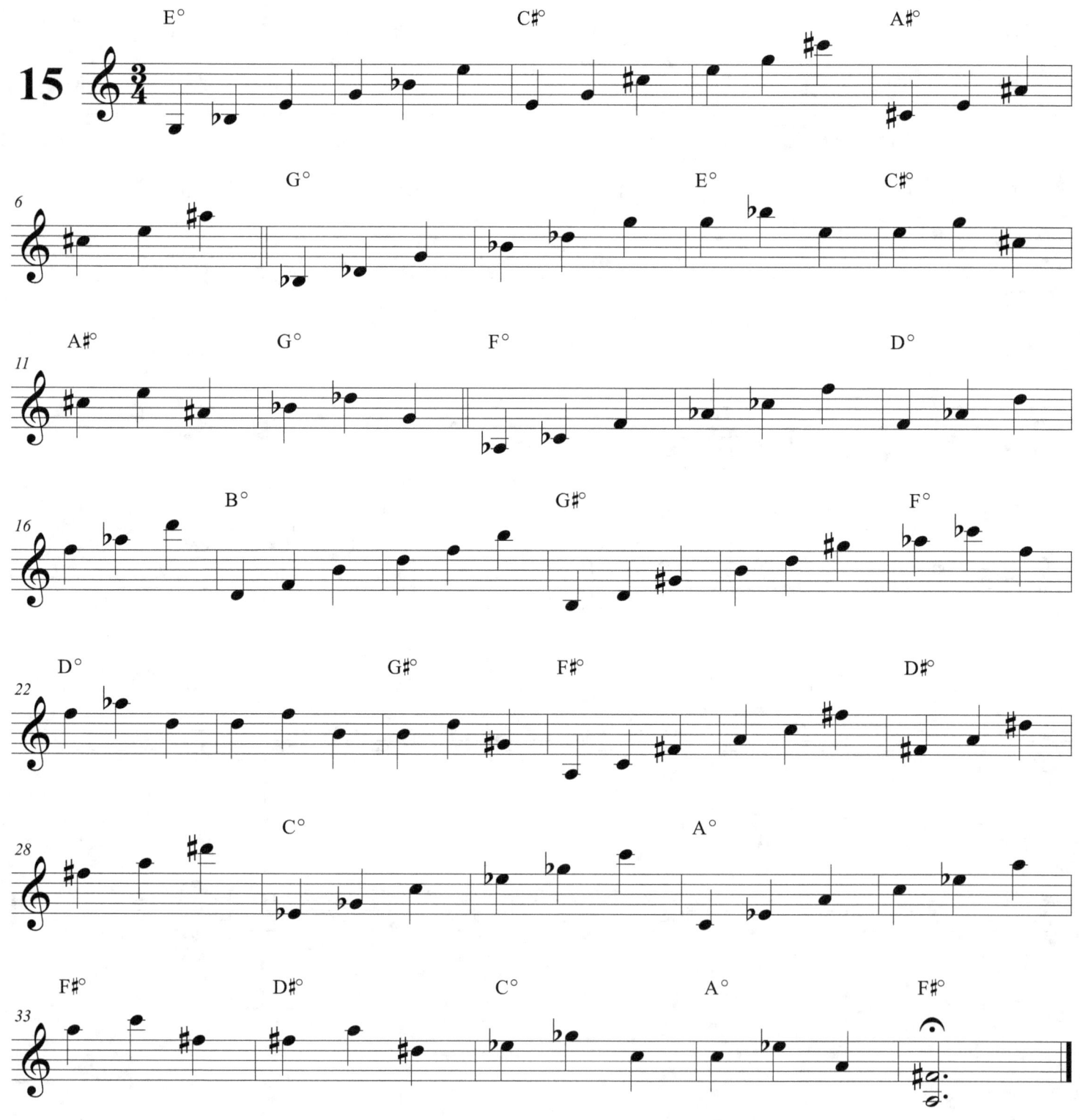

Etude 3-5-1
Augmented

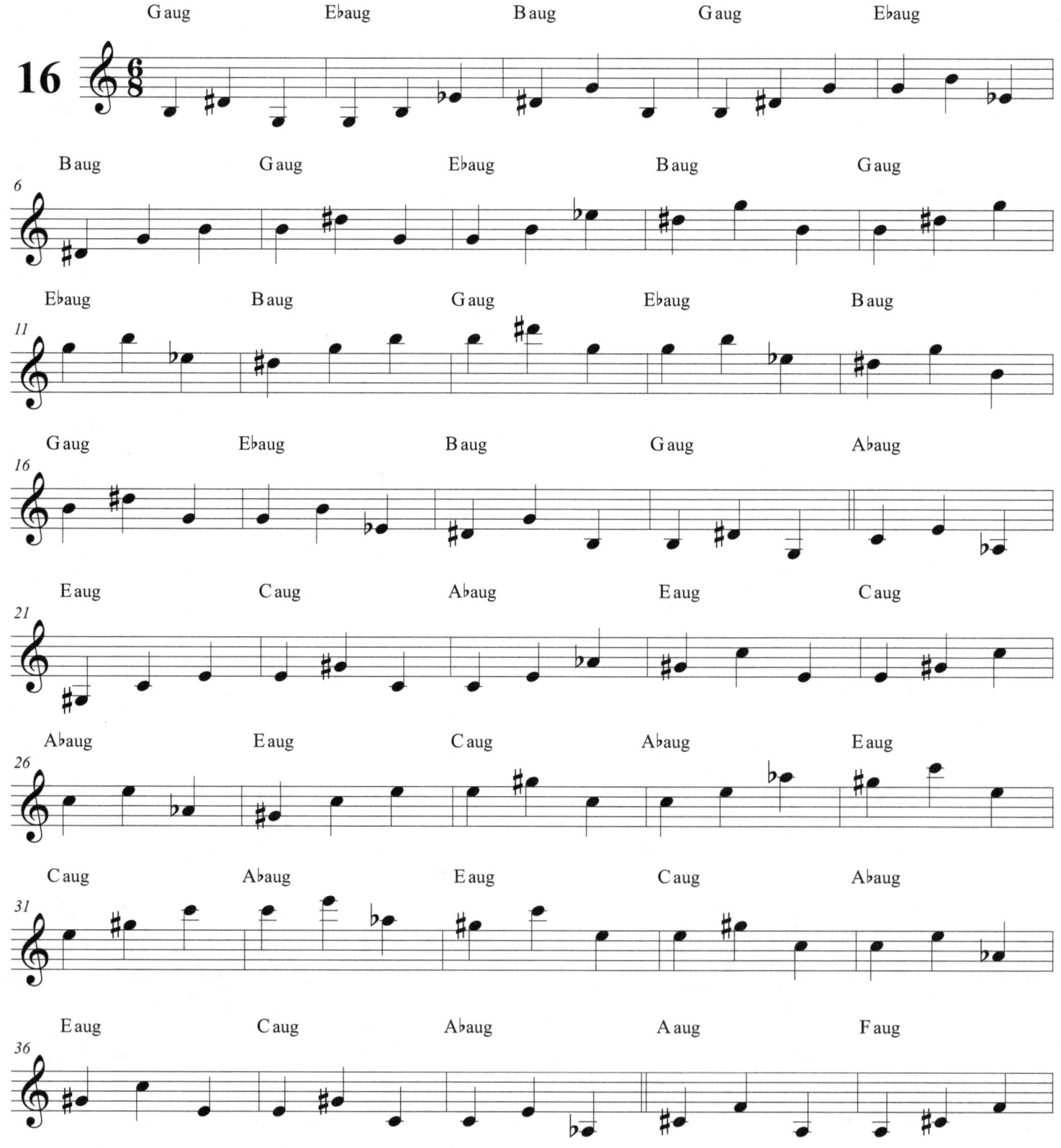

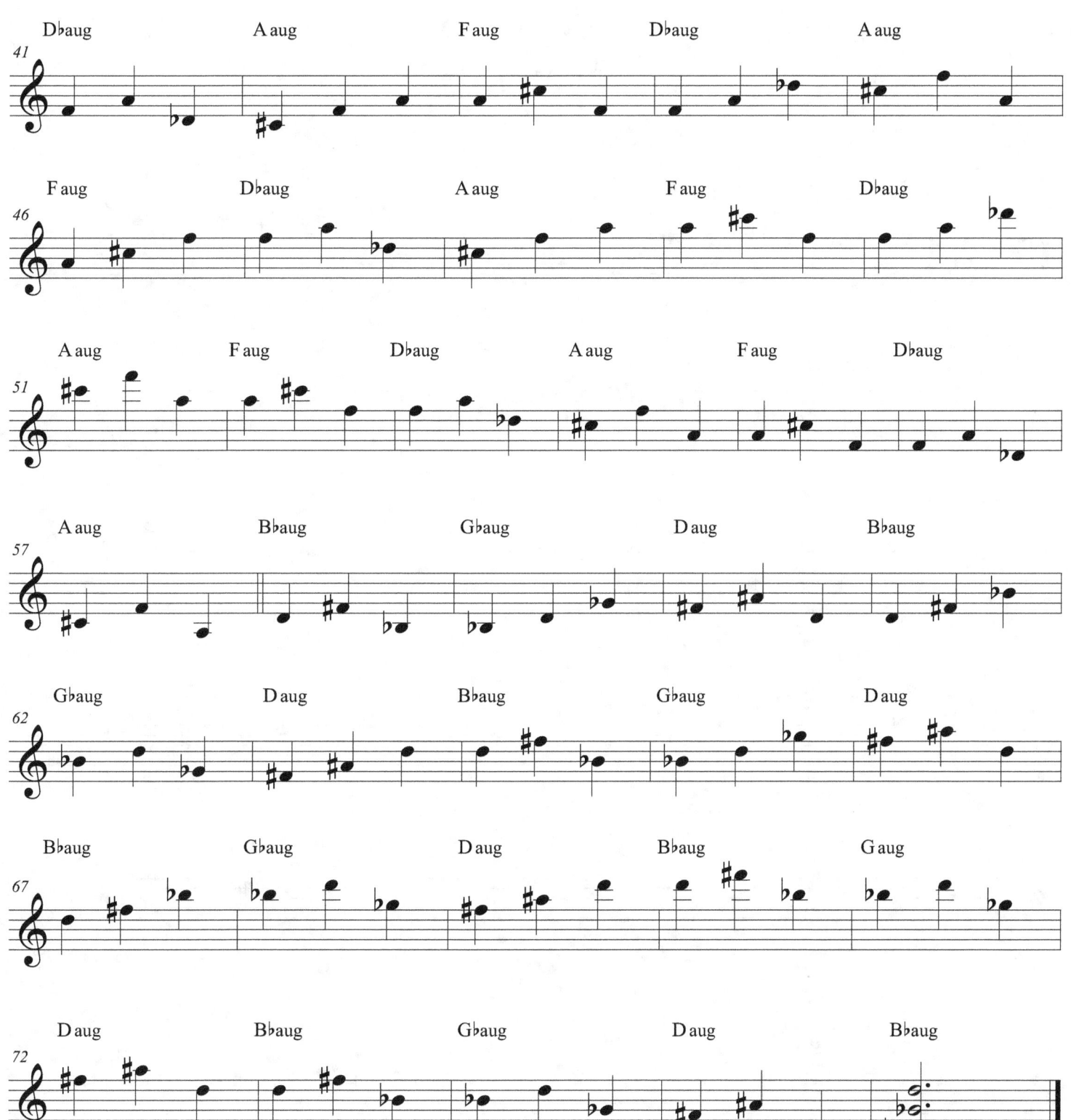

Etude 5-1-3
Major

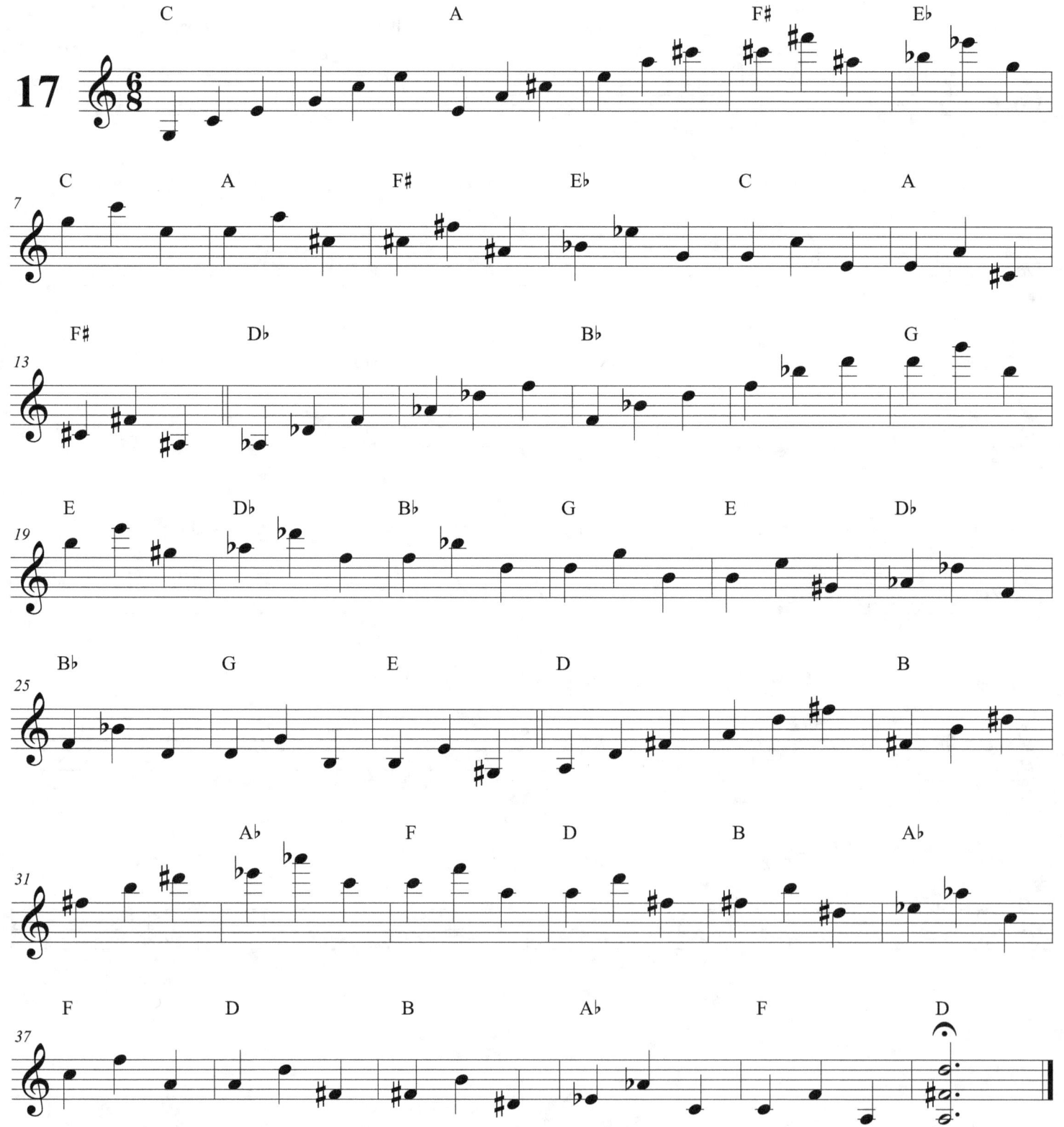

Etude 5-1-3
Minor

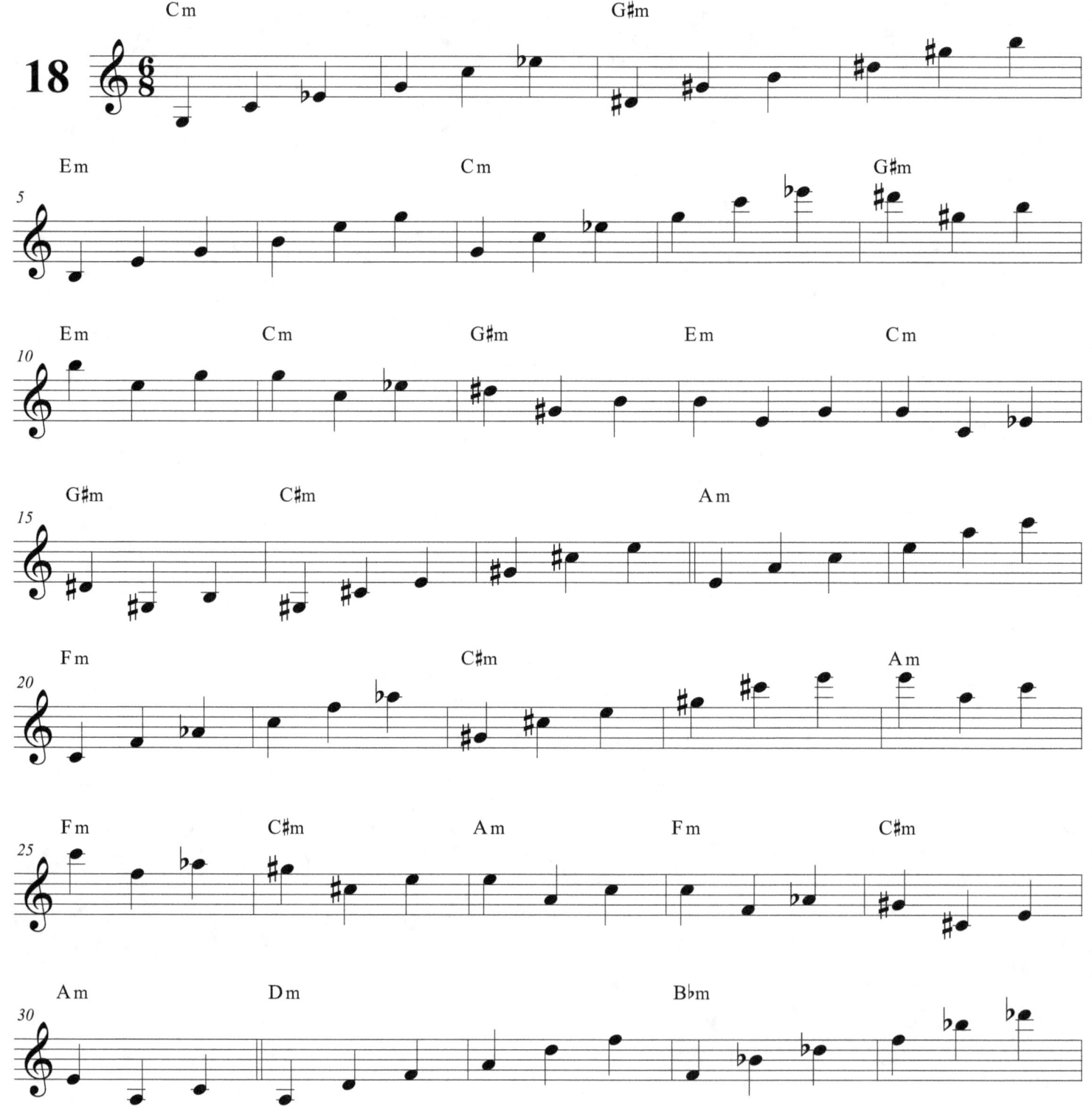

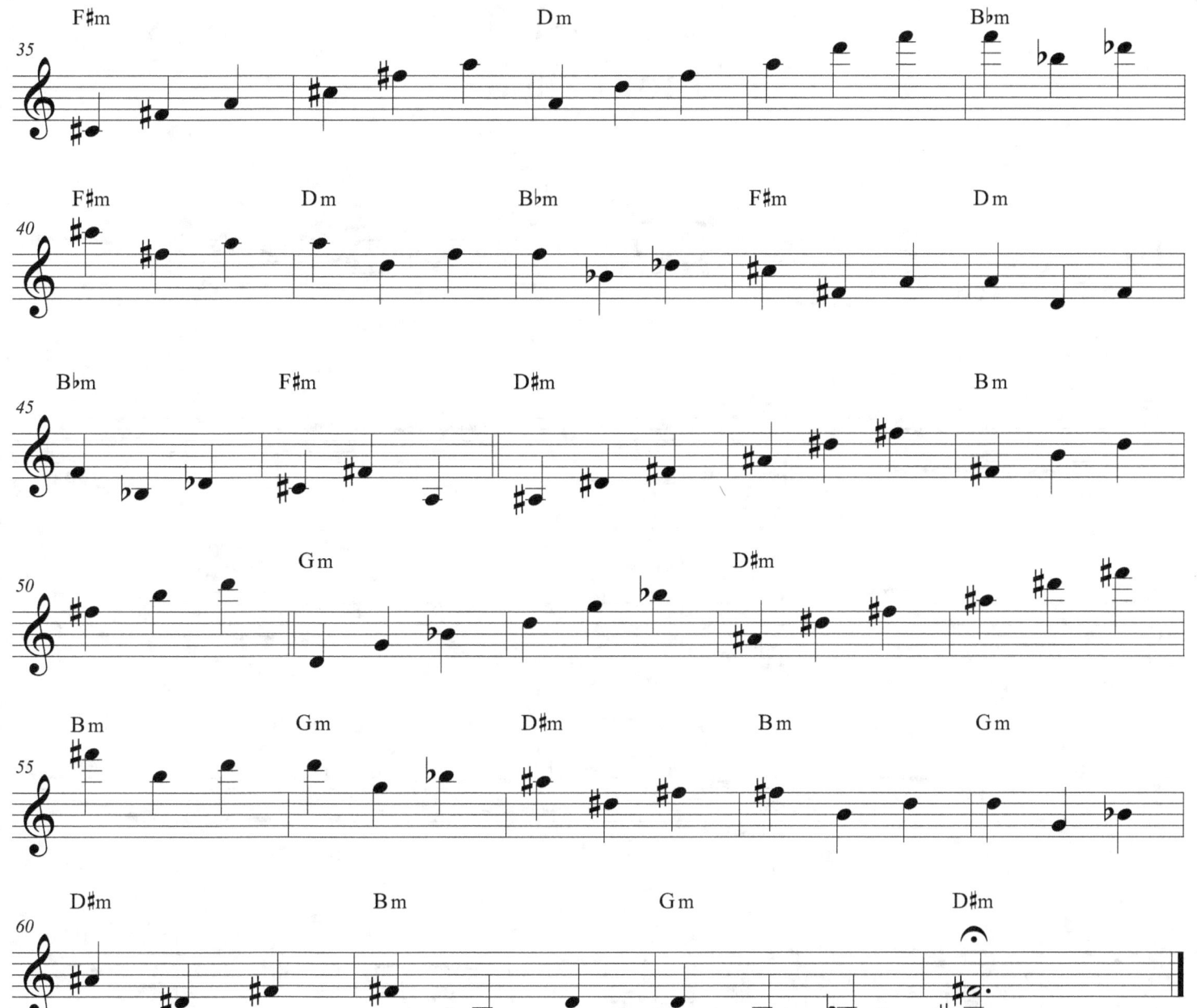

Etude 5-1-3
Diminished

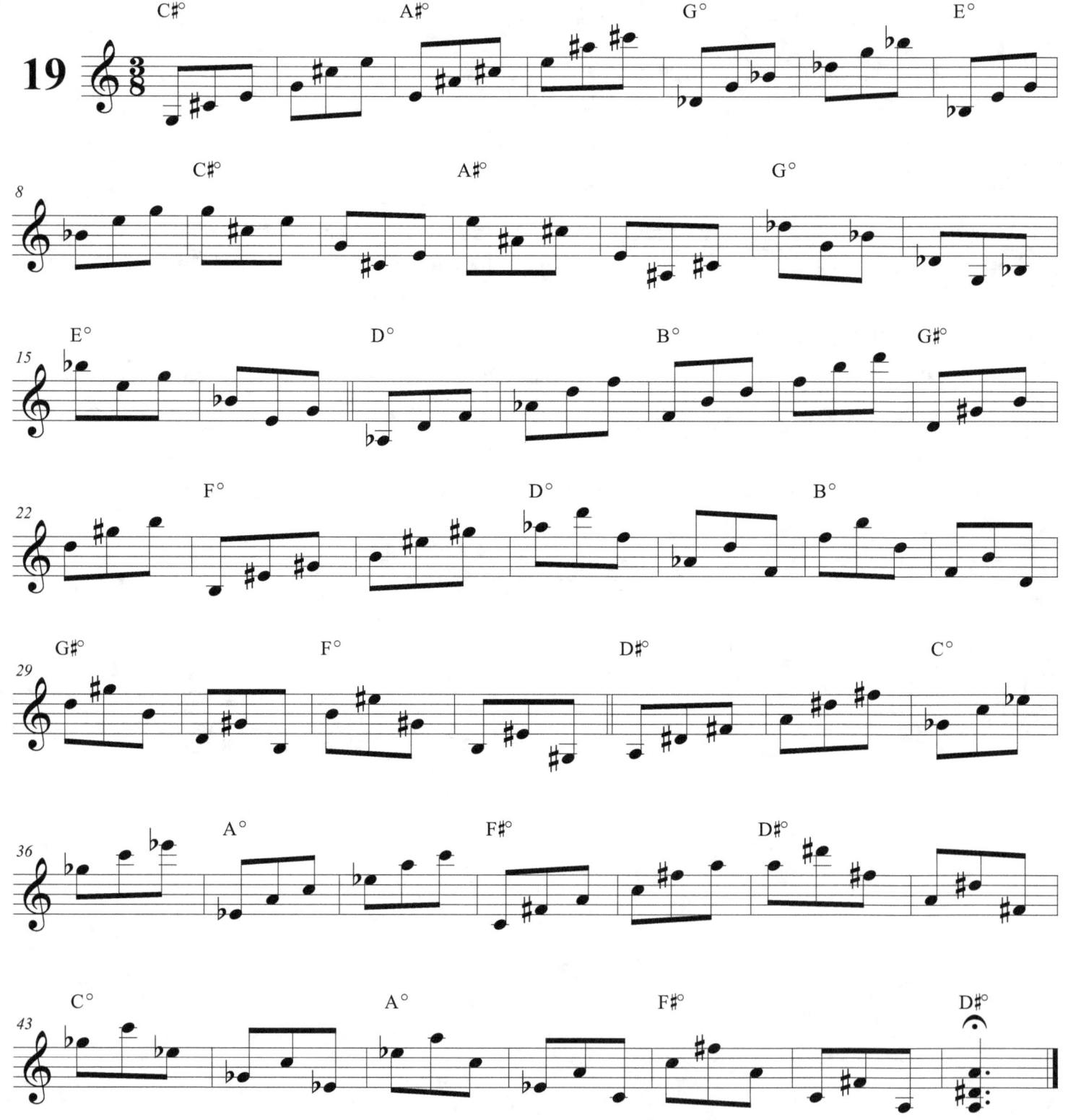

Etude 5-1-3
Augmented

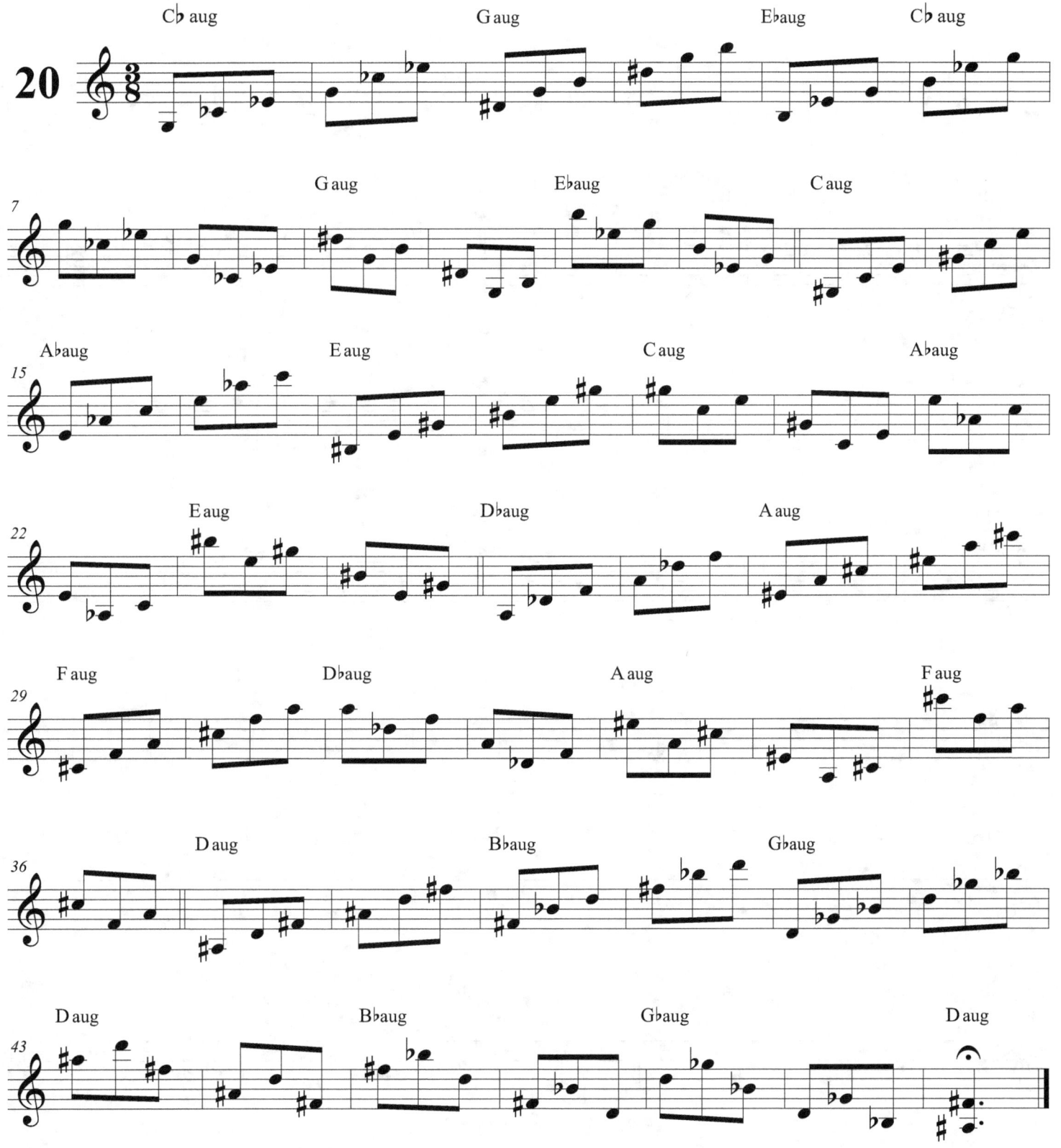

Exercise 5-3-1
Major

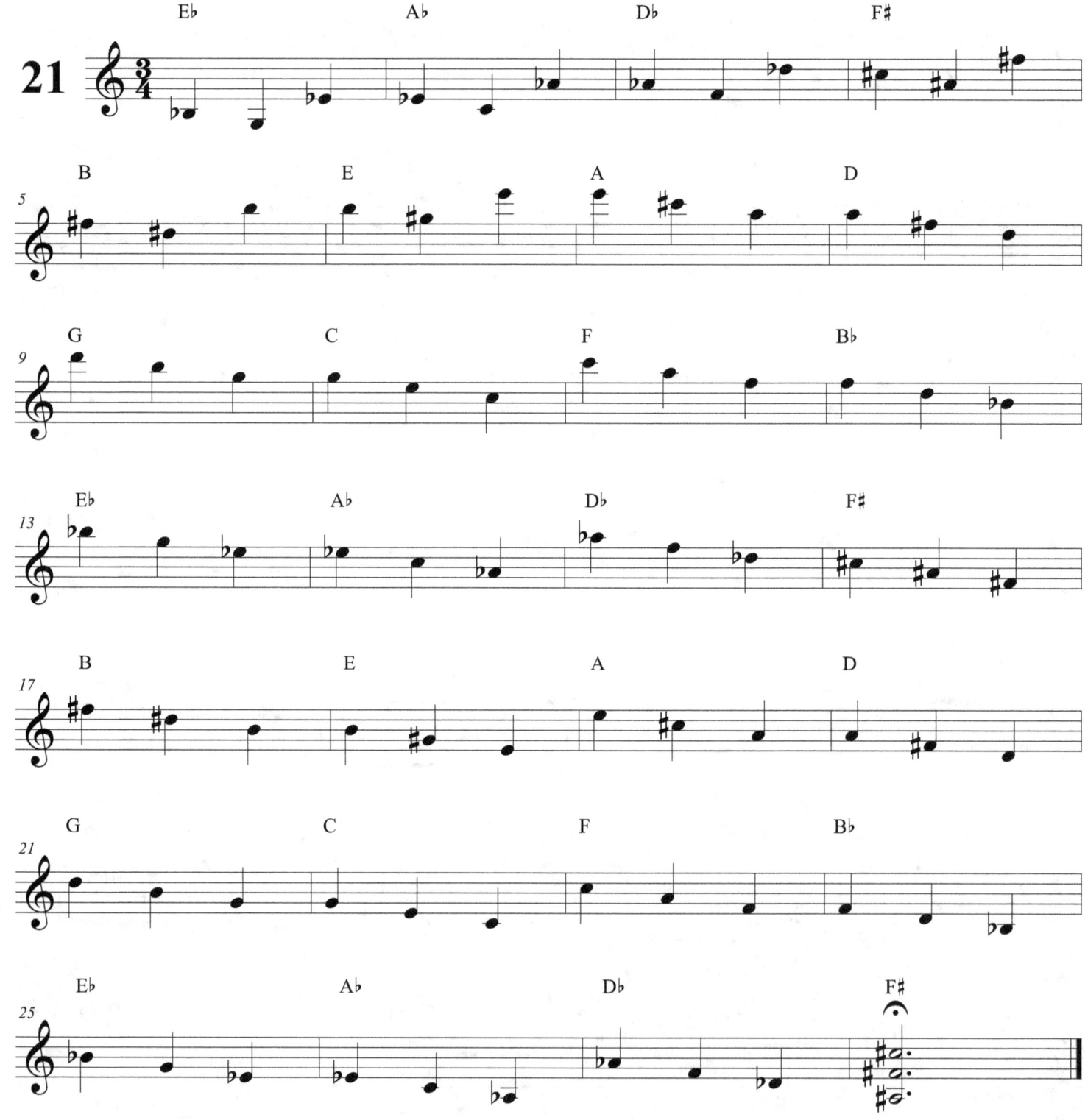

Etude 5-3-1
Minor

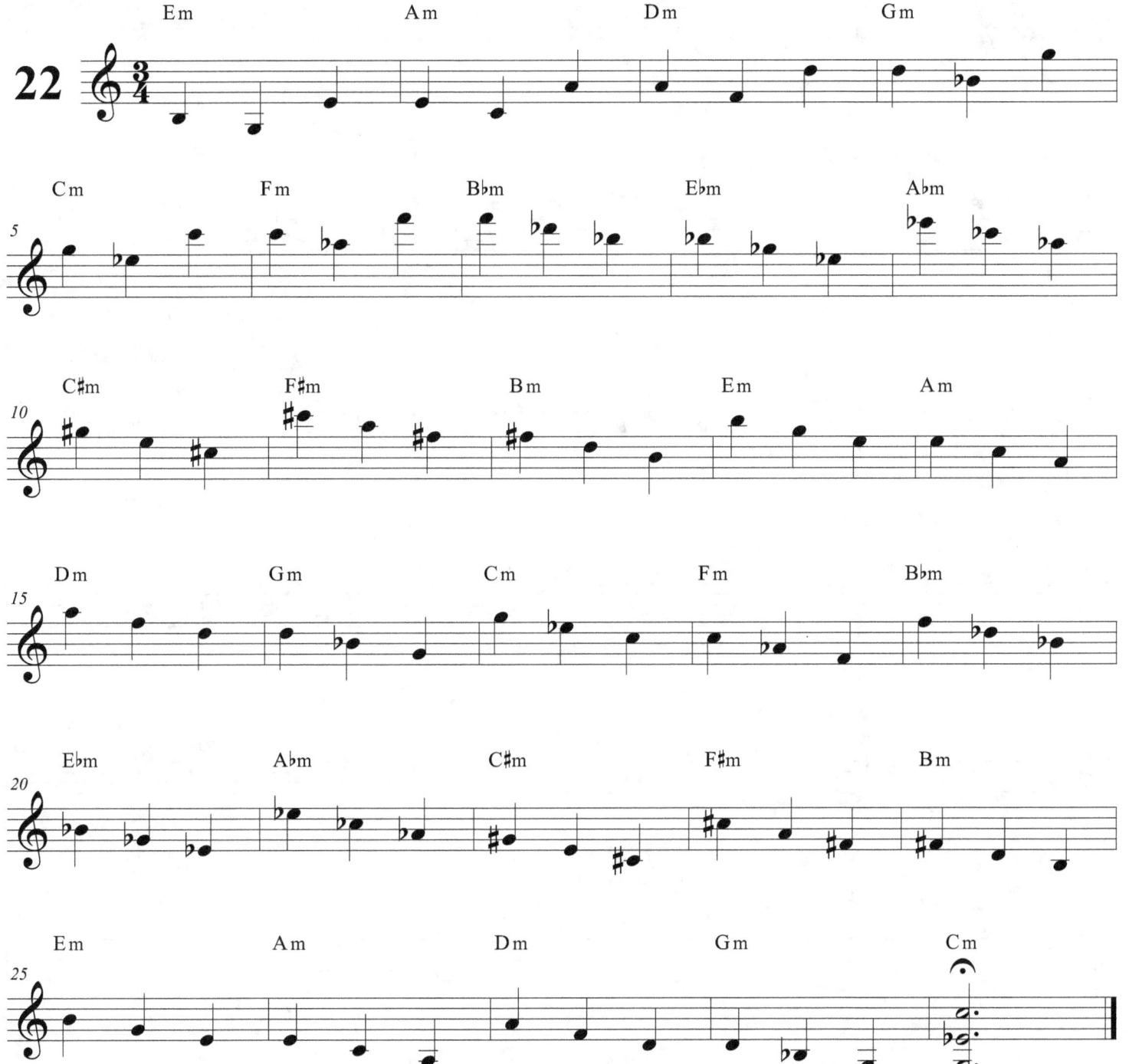

Etude 5-3-1
Diminished

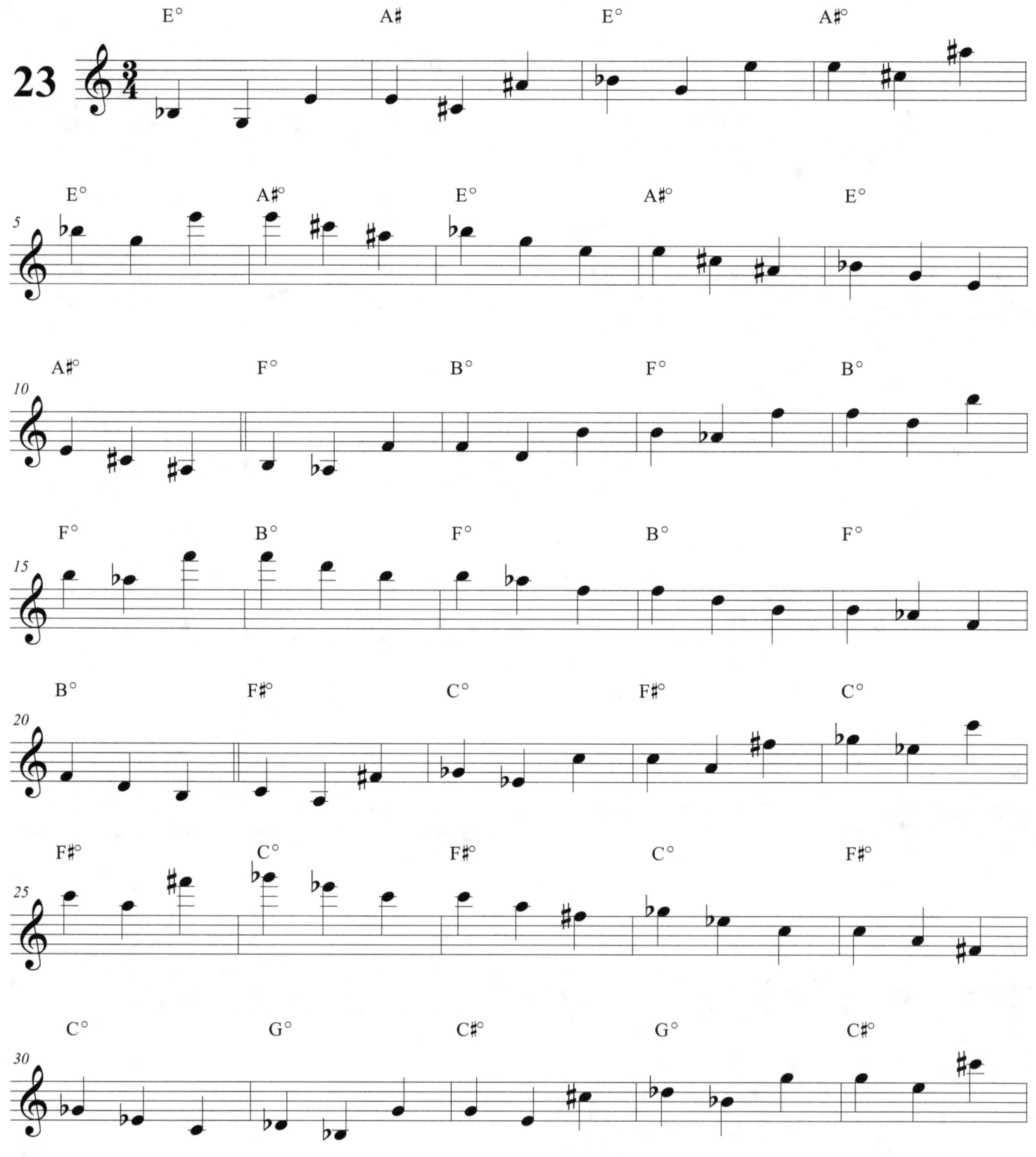

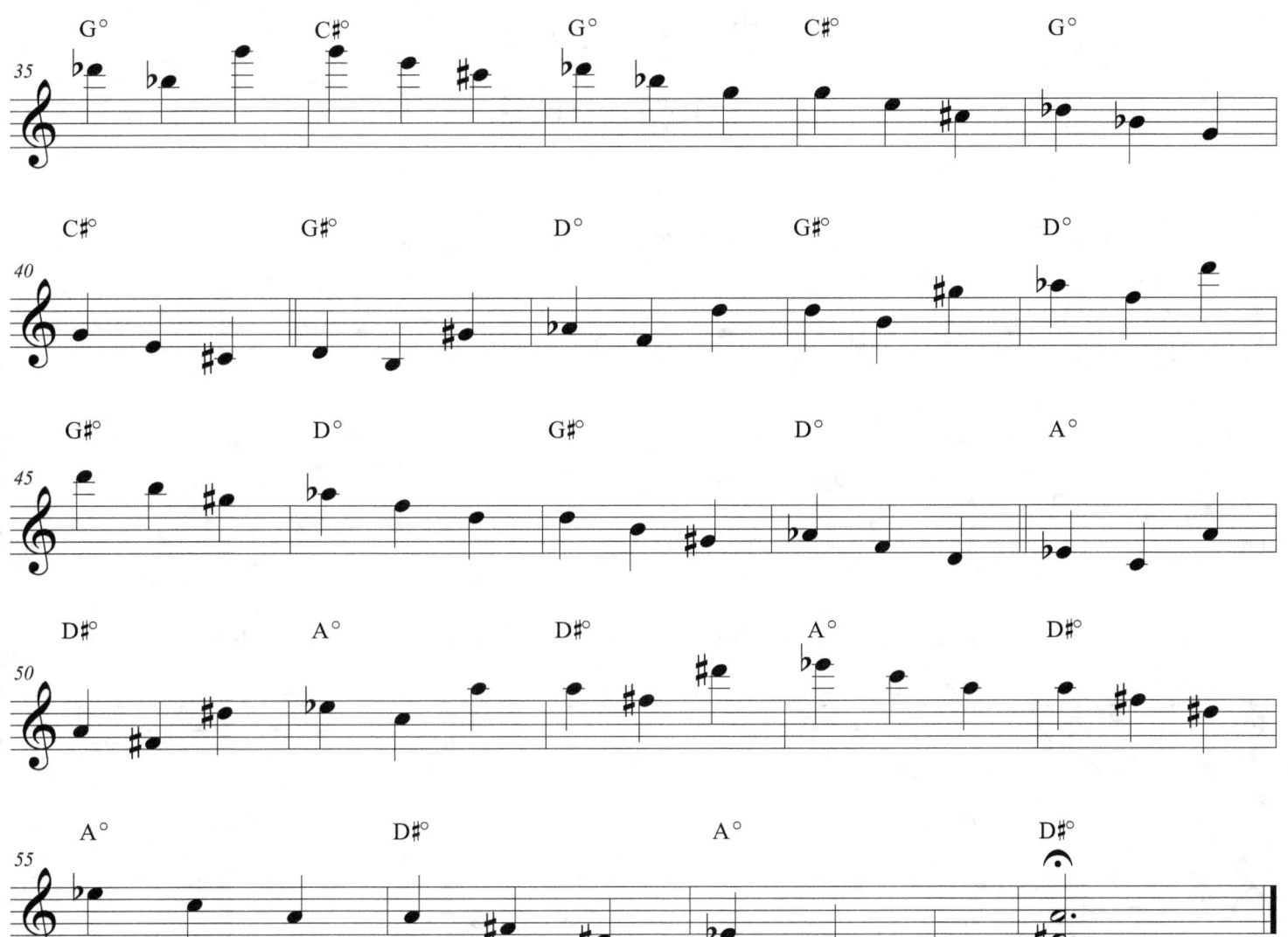

Etude 5-3-1
Augmented

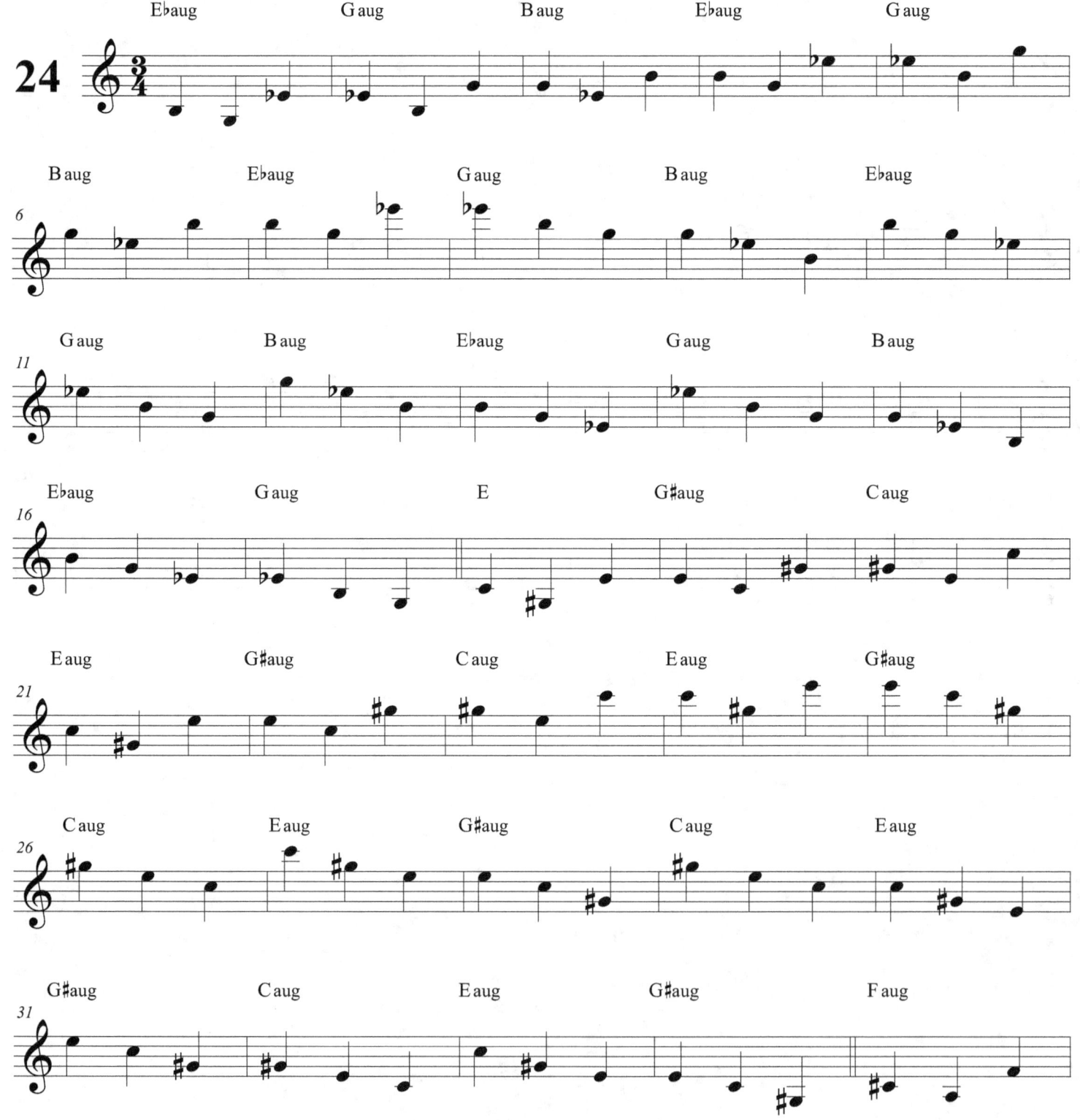

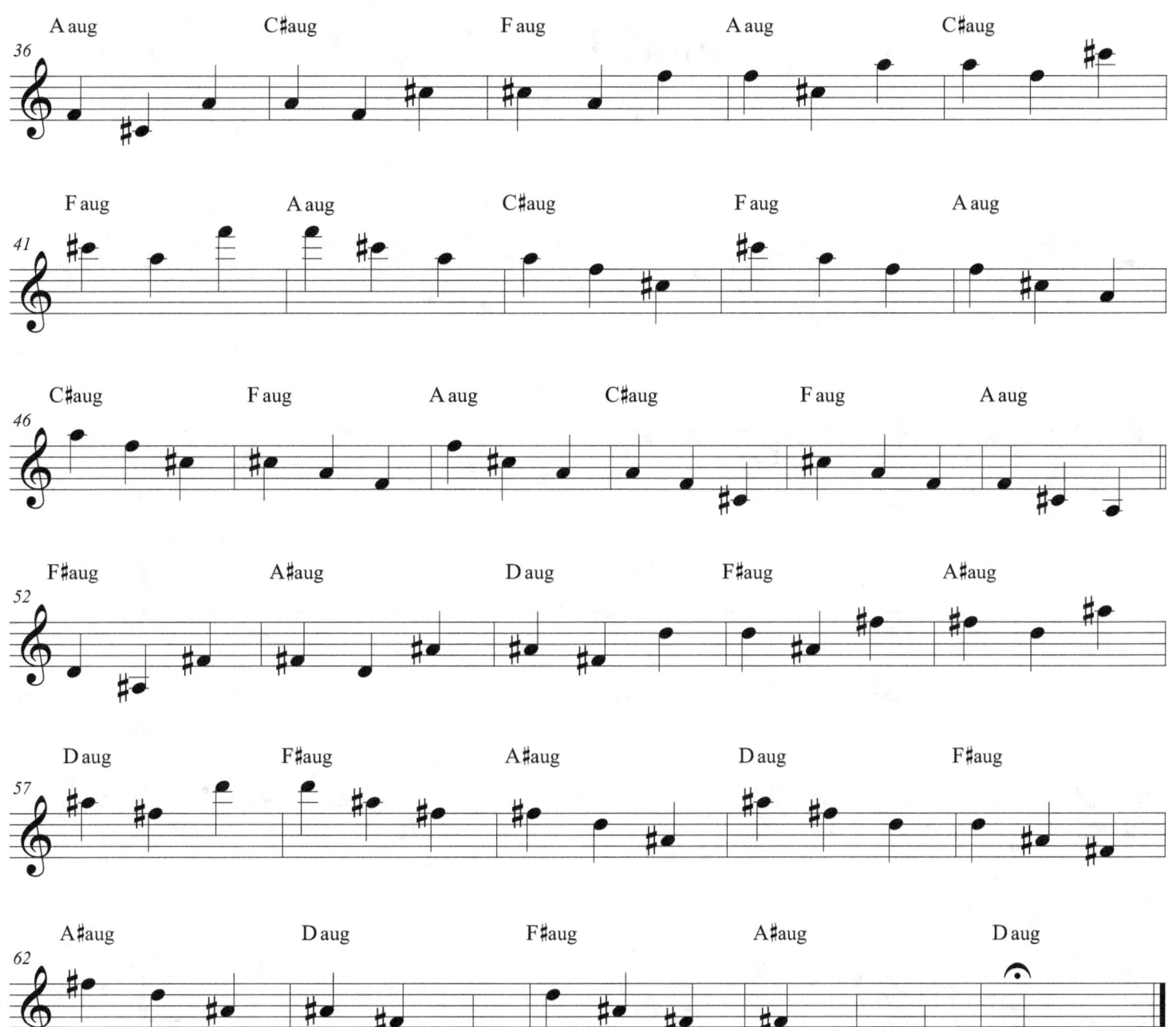

Etude 1-3-1-5
Major

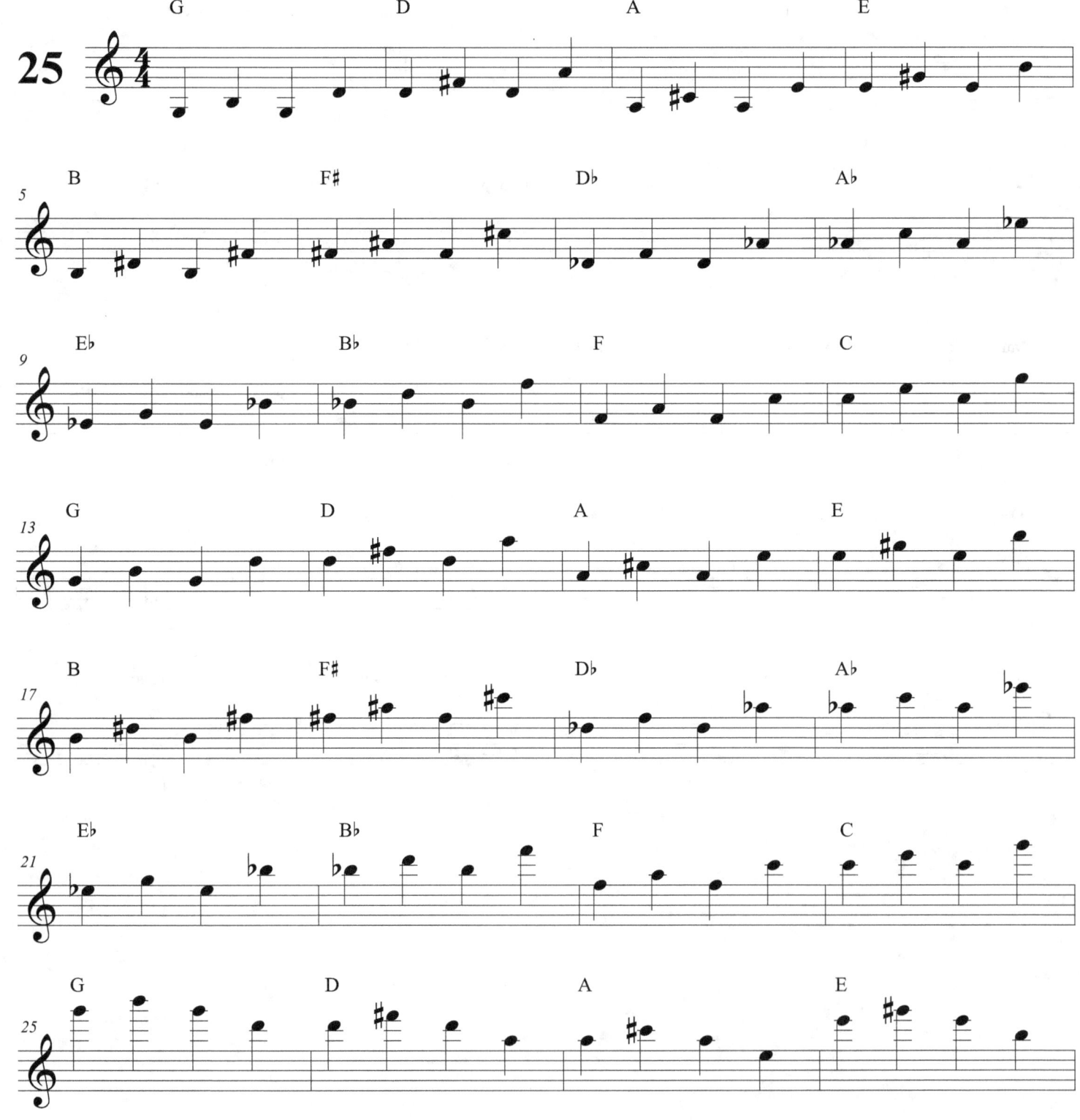

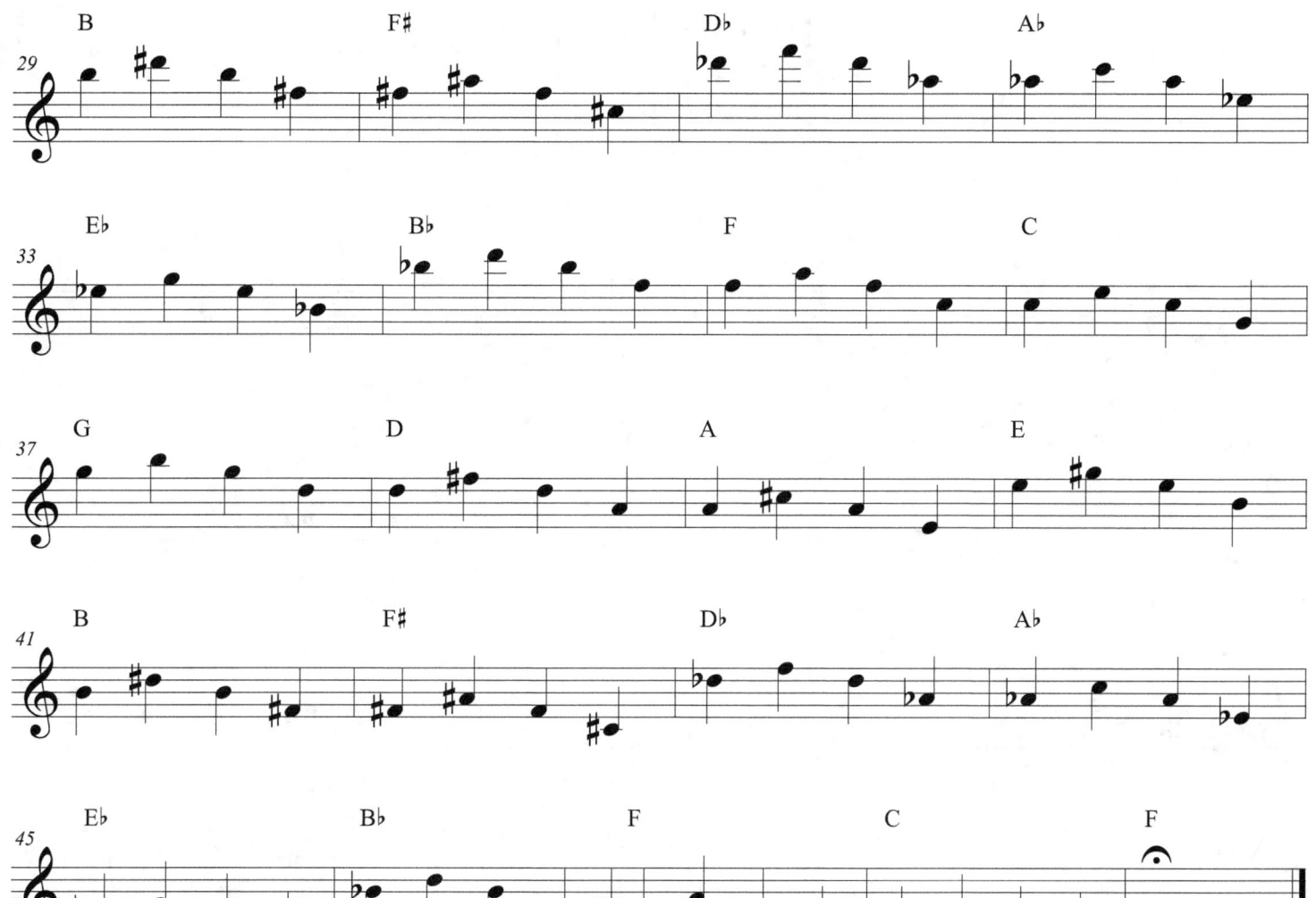

Etude 1-3-1-5
Minor

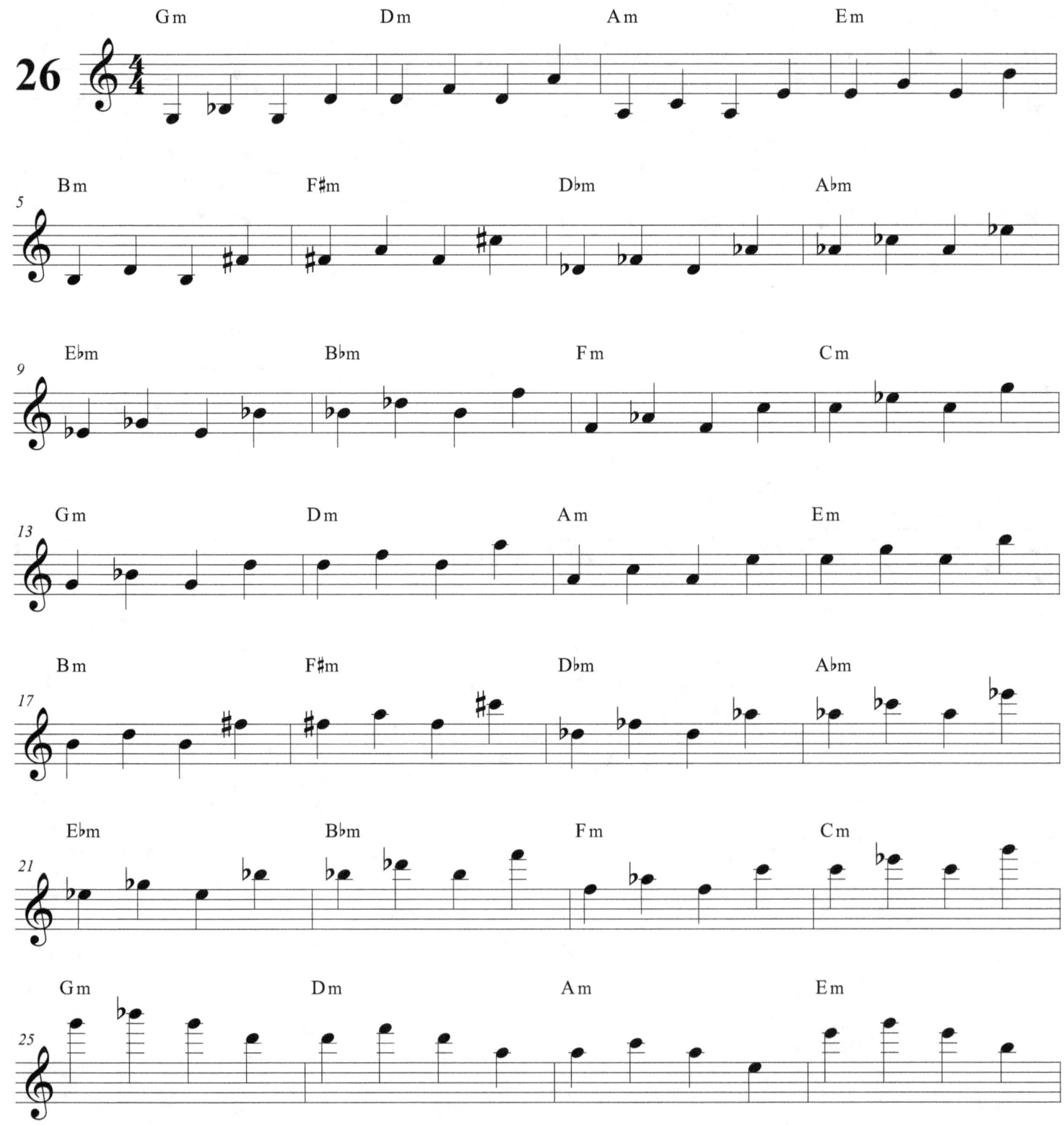

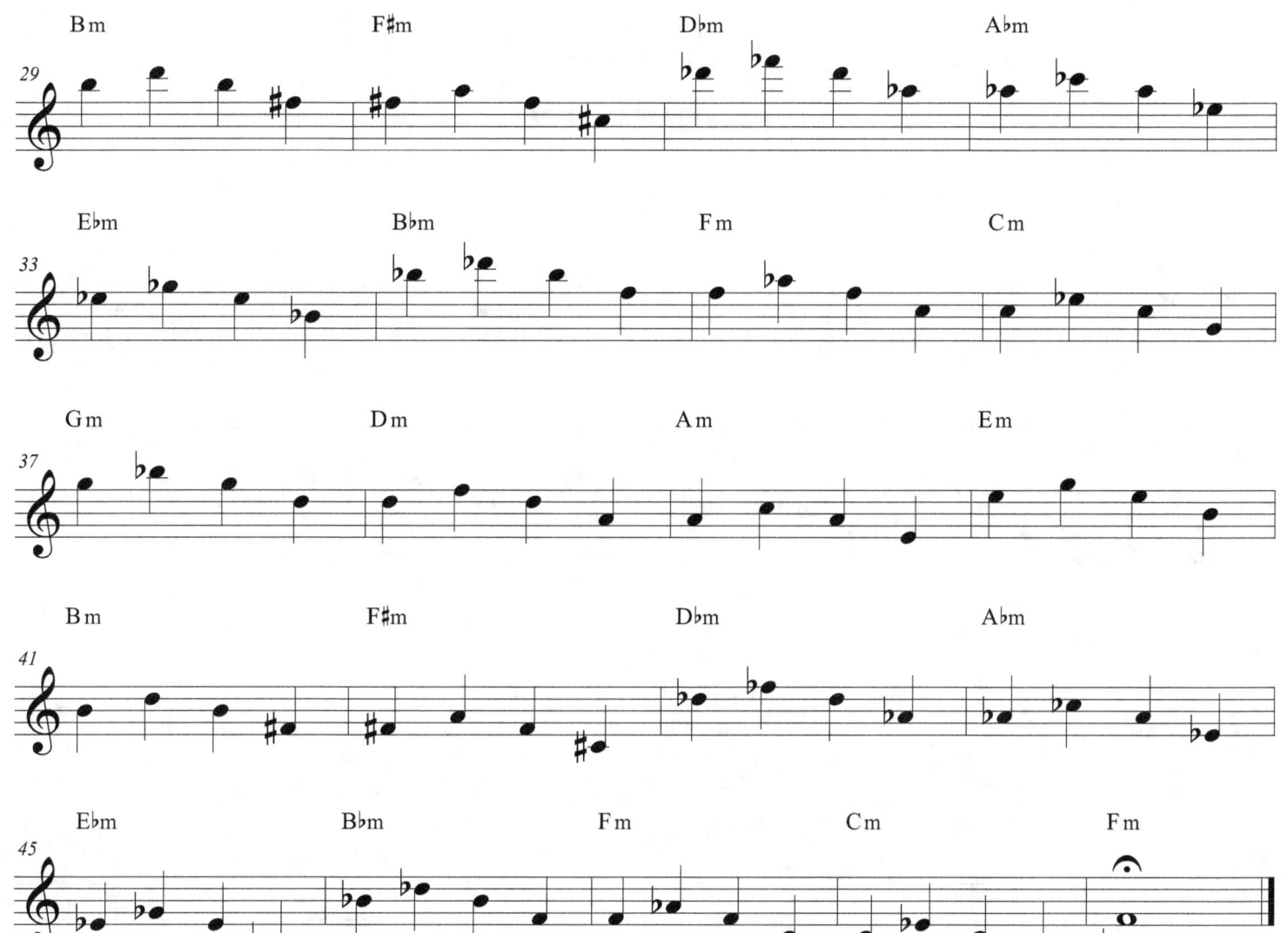

Etude 1-3-1-5
Diminished

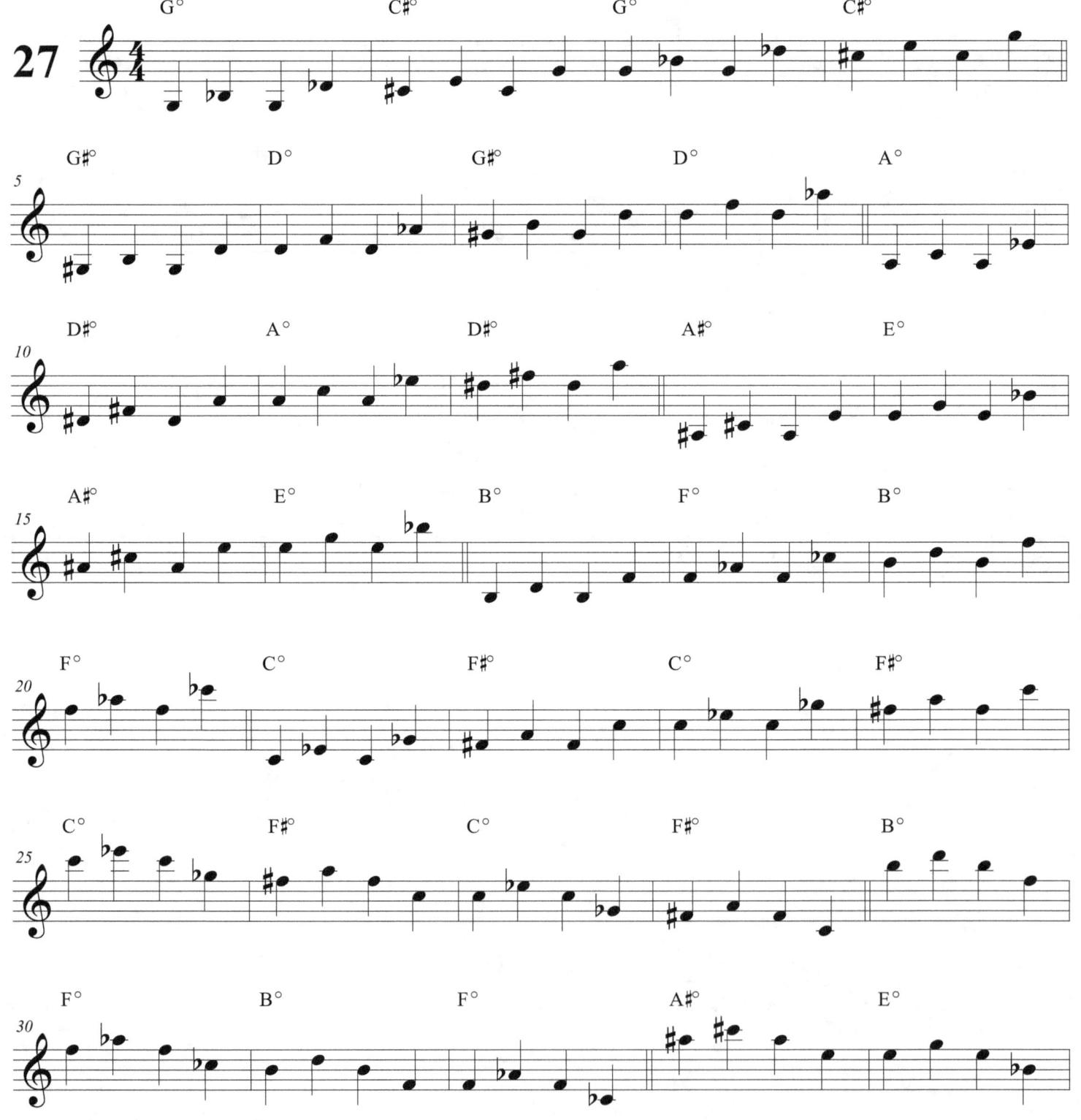

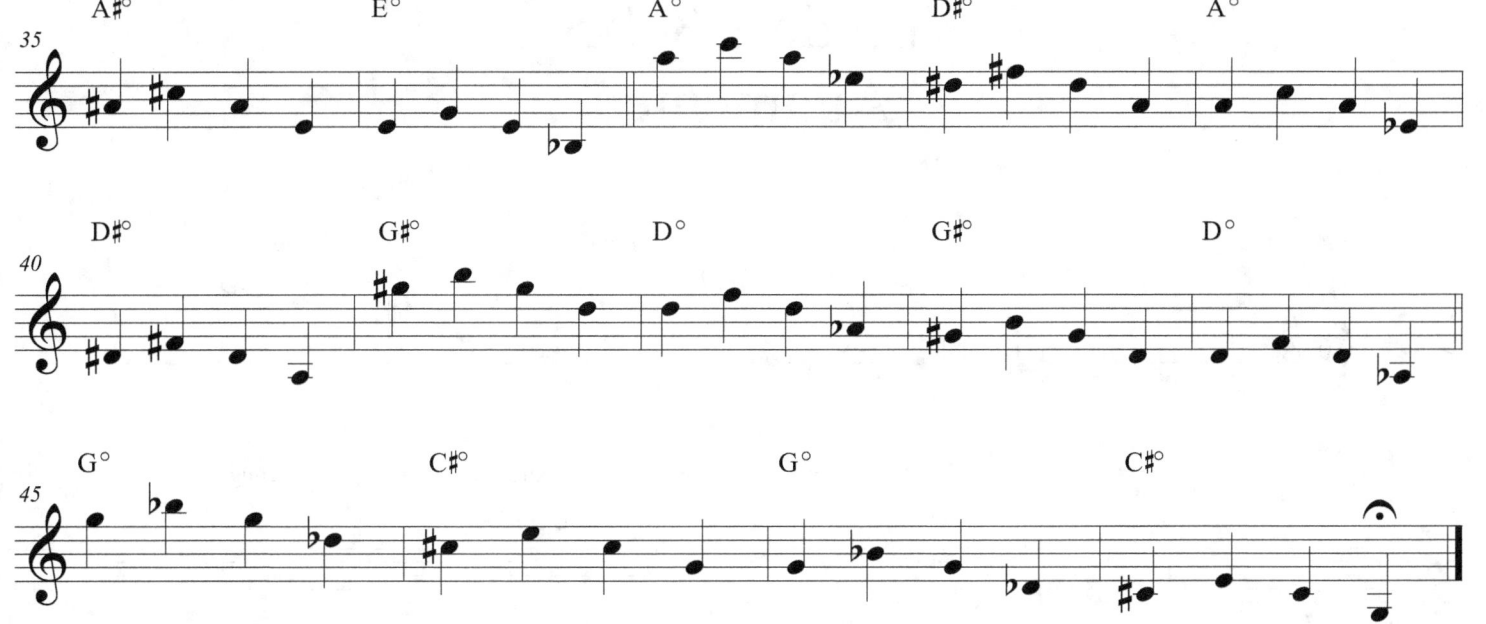

Etude 1-3-1-5
Augmented

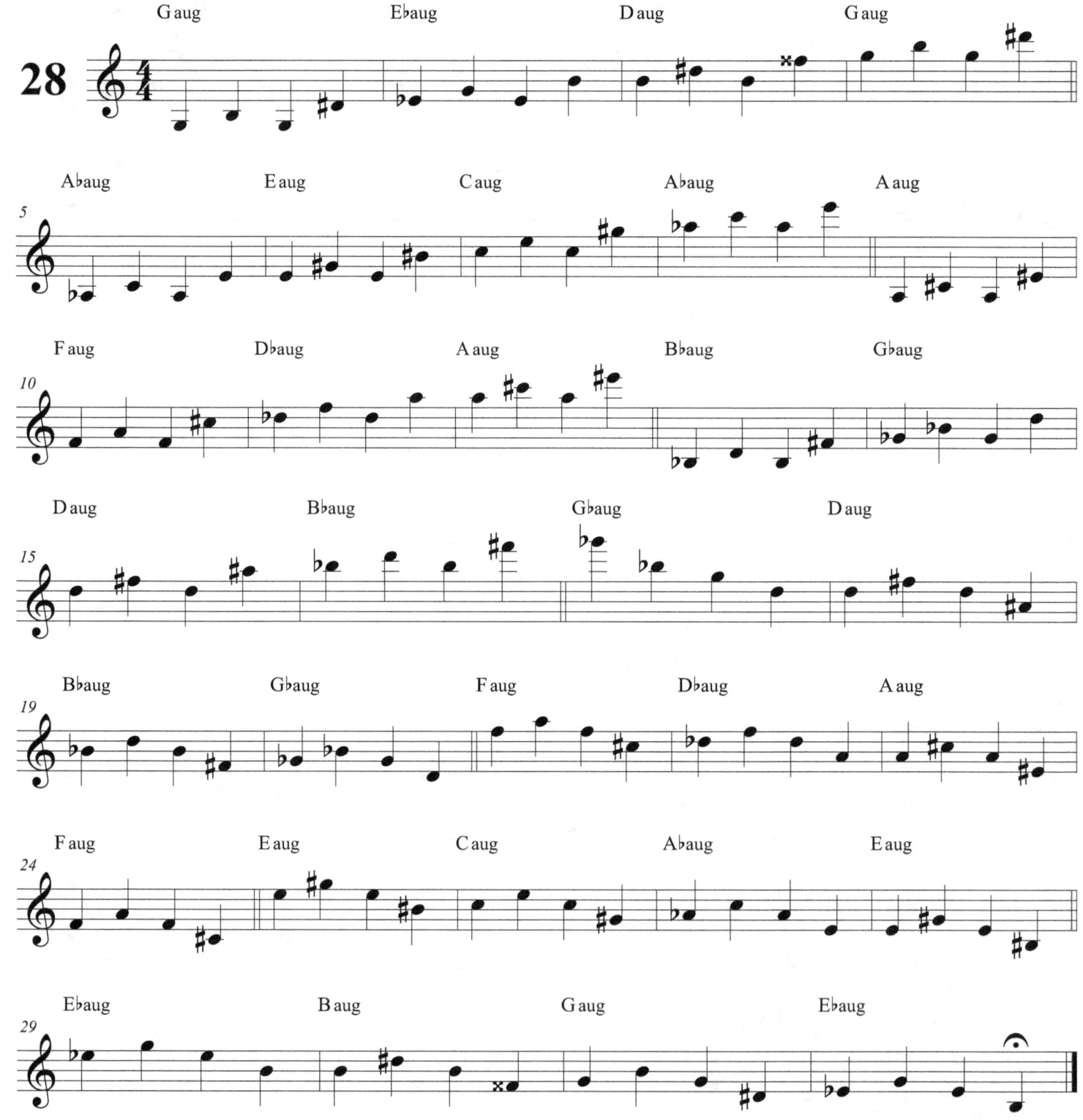

Etude 1-5-1-3
Major

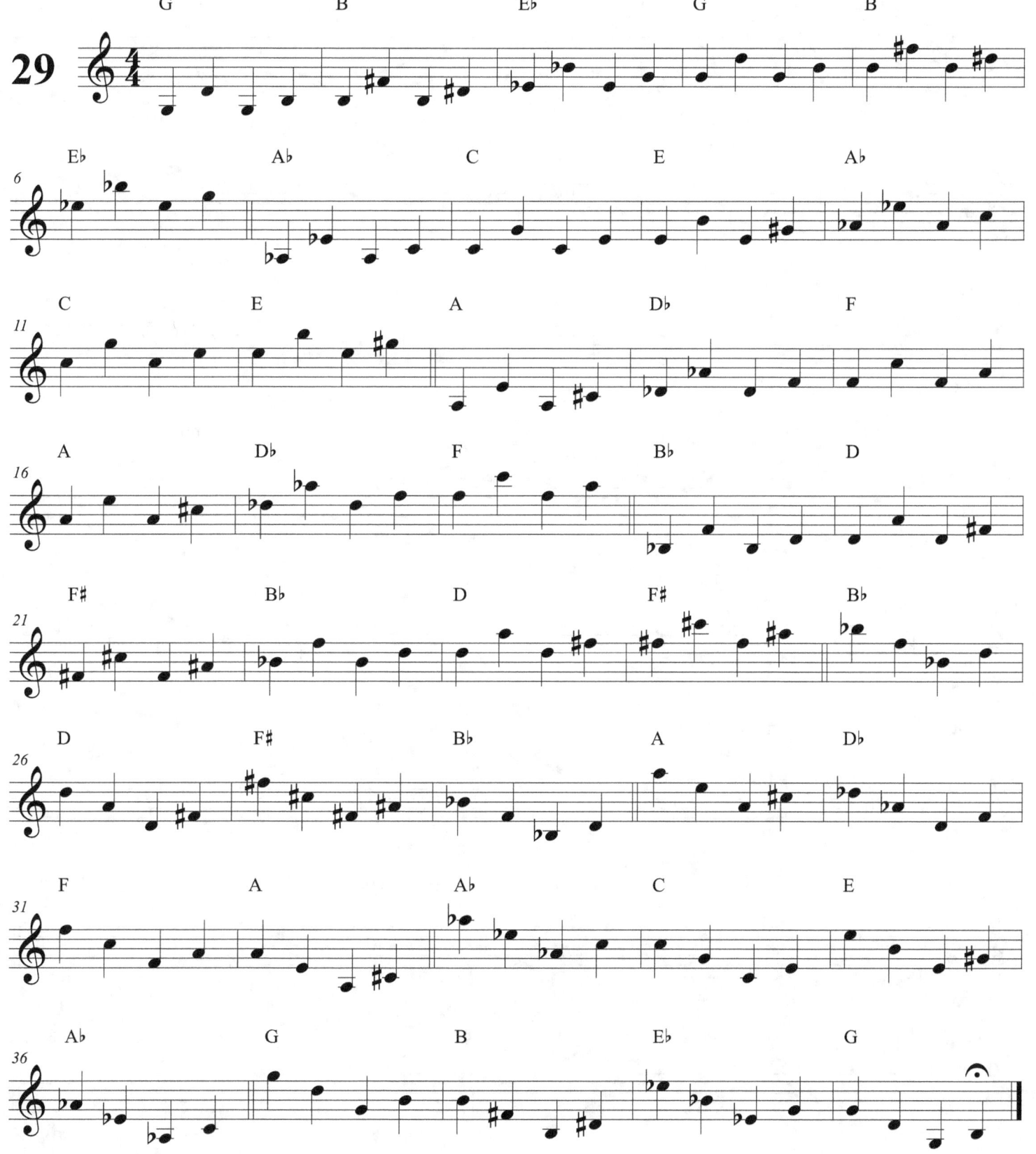

Etude 1-5-1-3
Minor

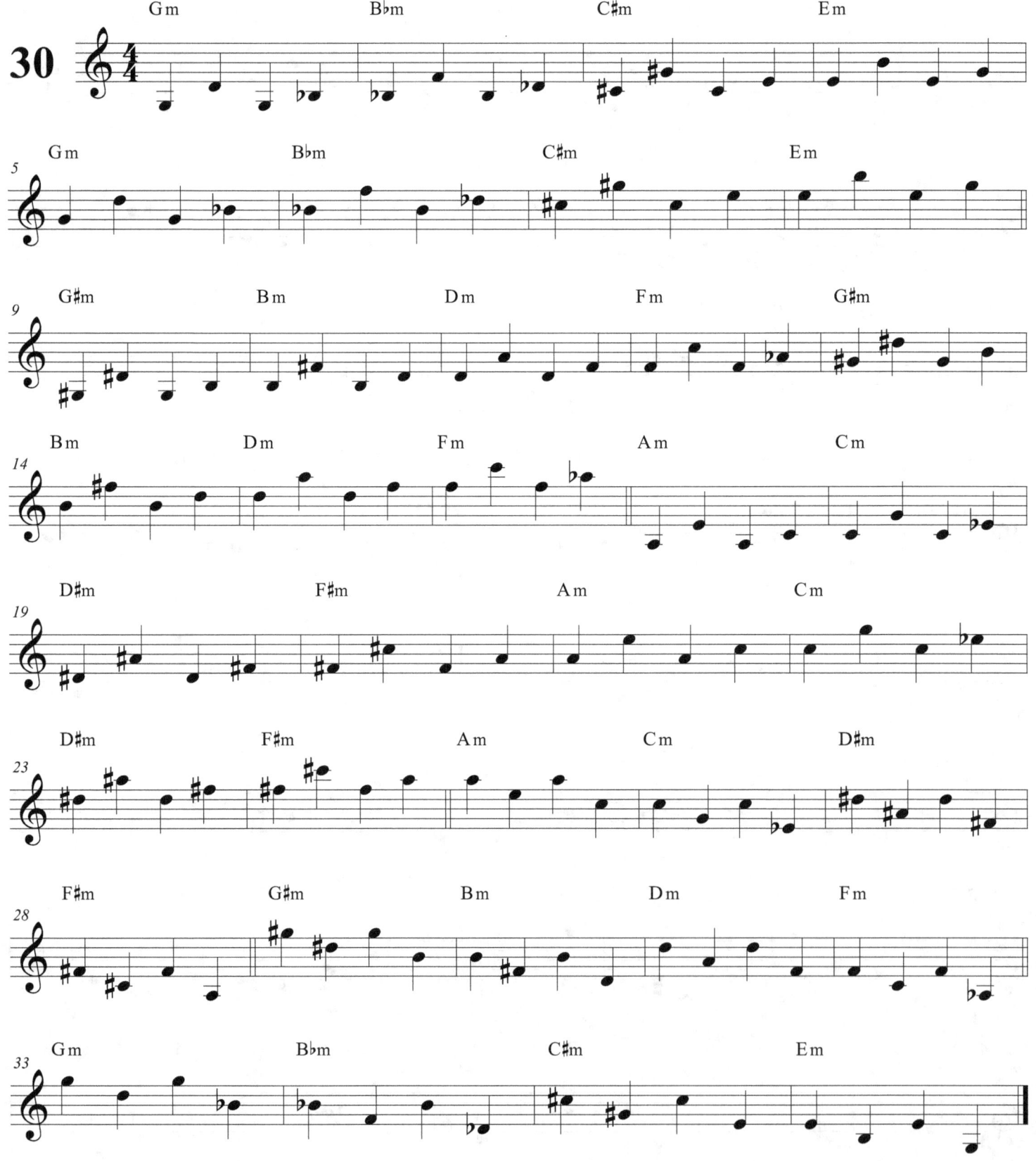

Etude 1-5-1-3
Diminished

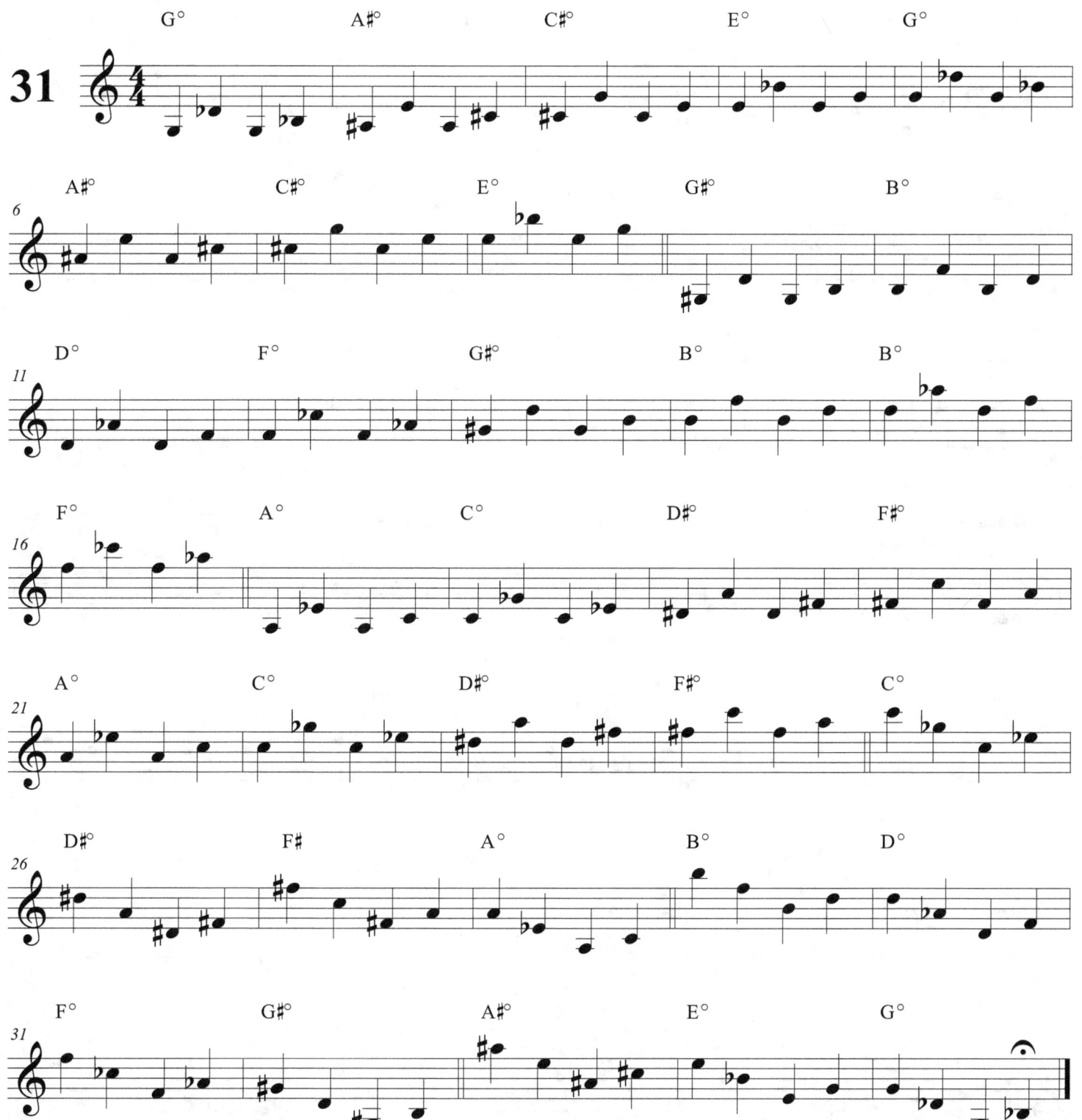

Etude 1-5-1-3
Augmented

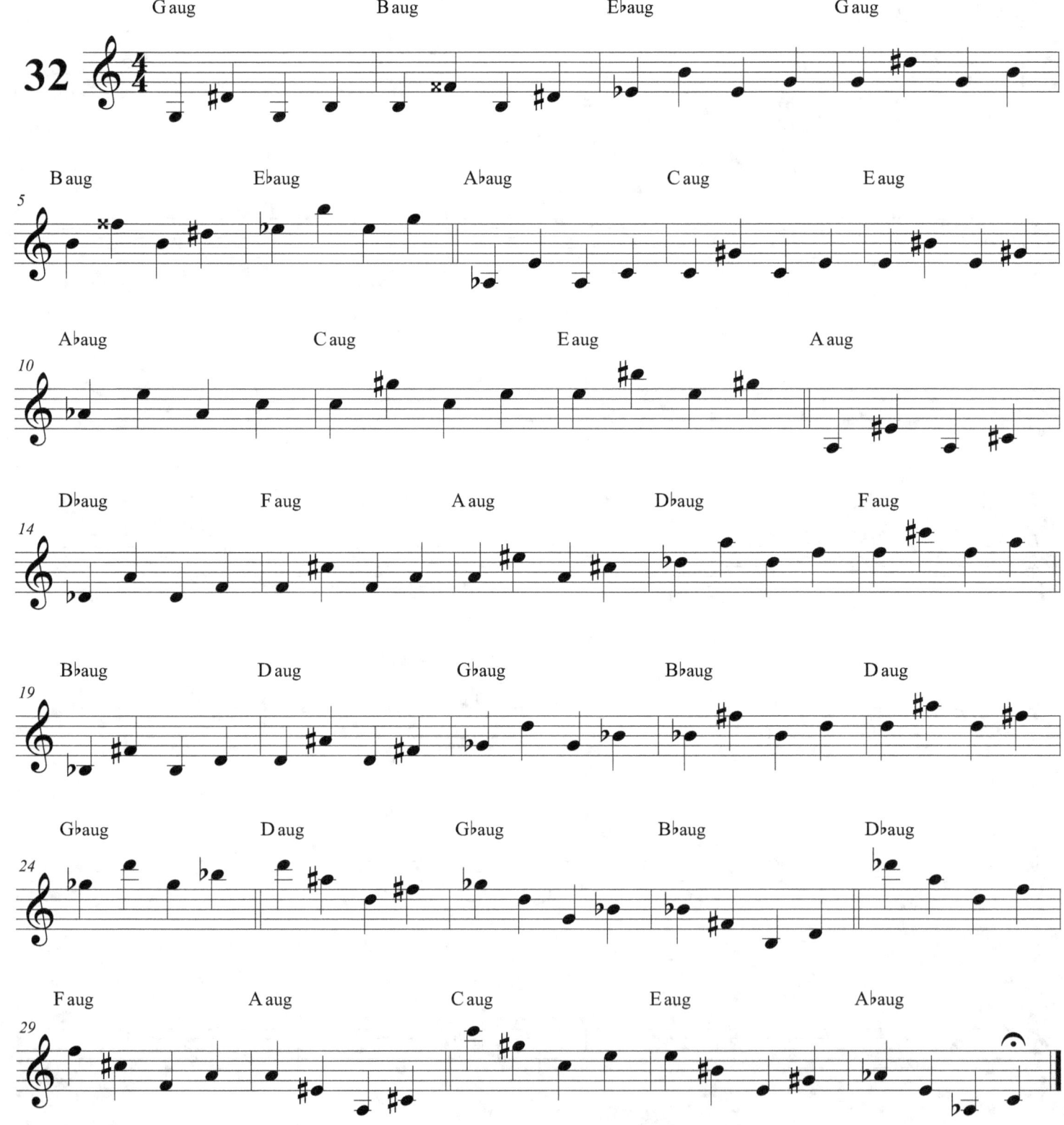

Etude 3-1-3-5
Major

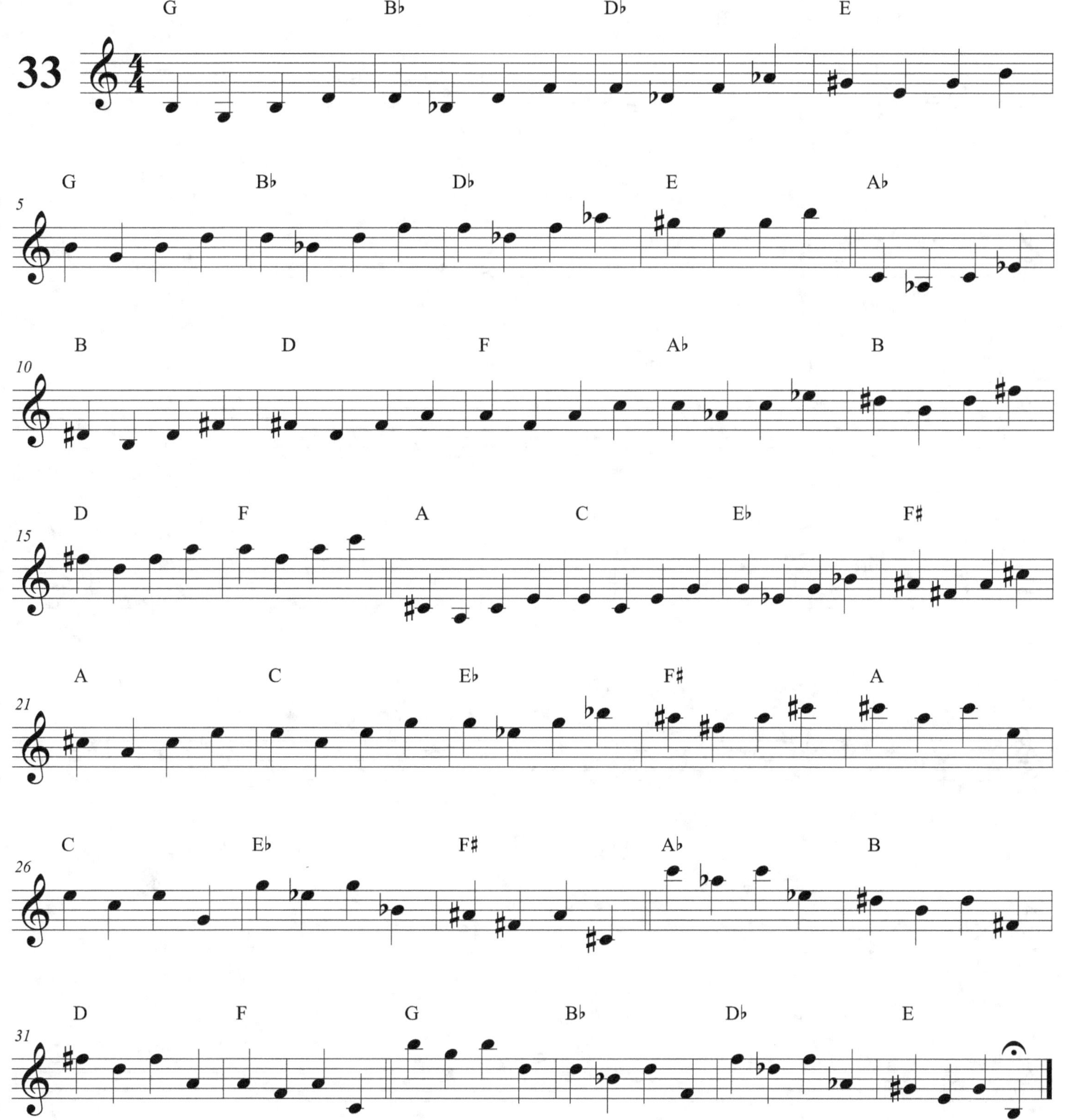

Etude 3-1-3-5
Minor

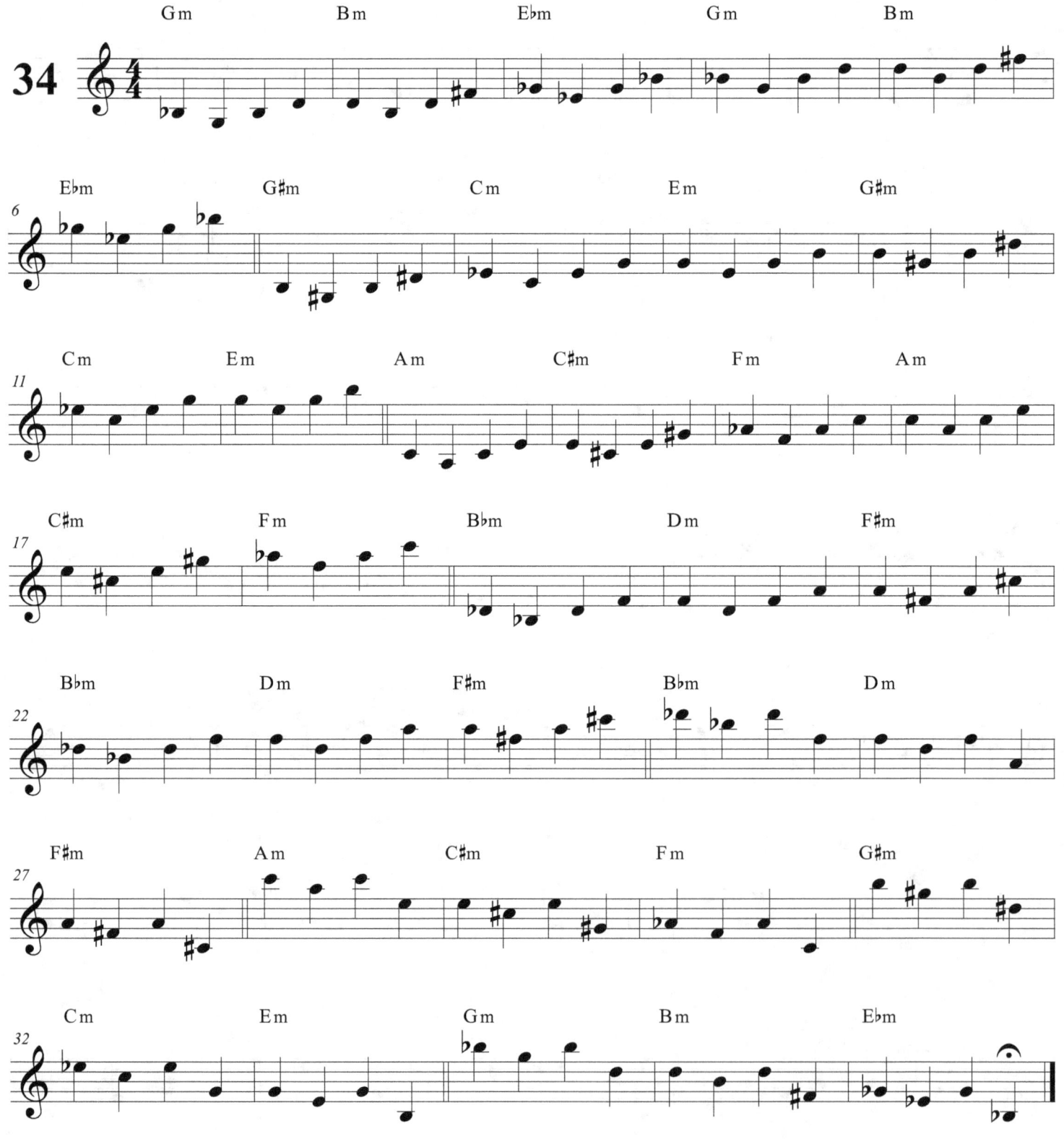

Etude 3-1-3-5
Diminished

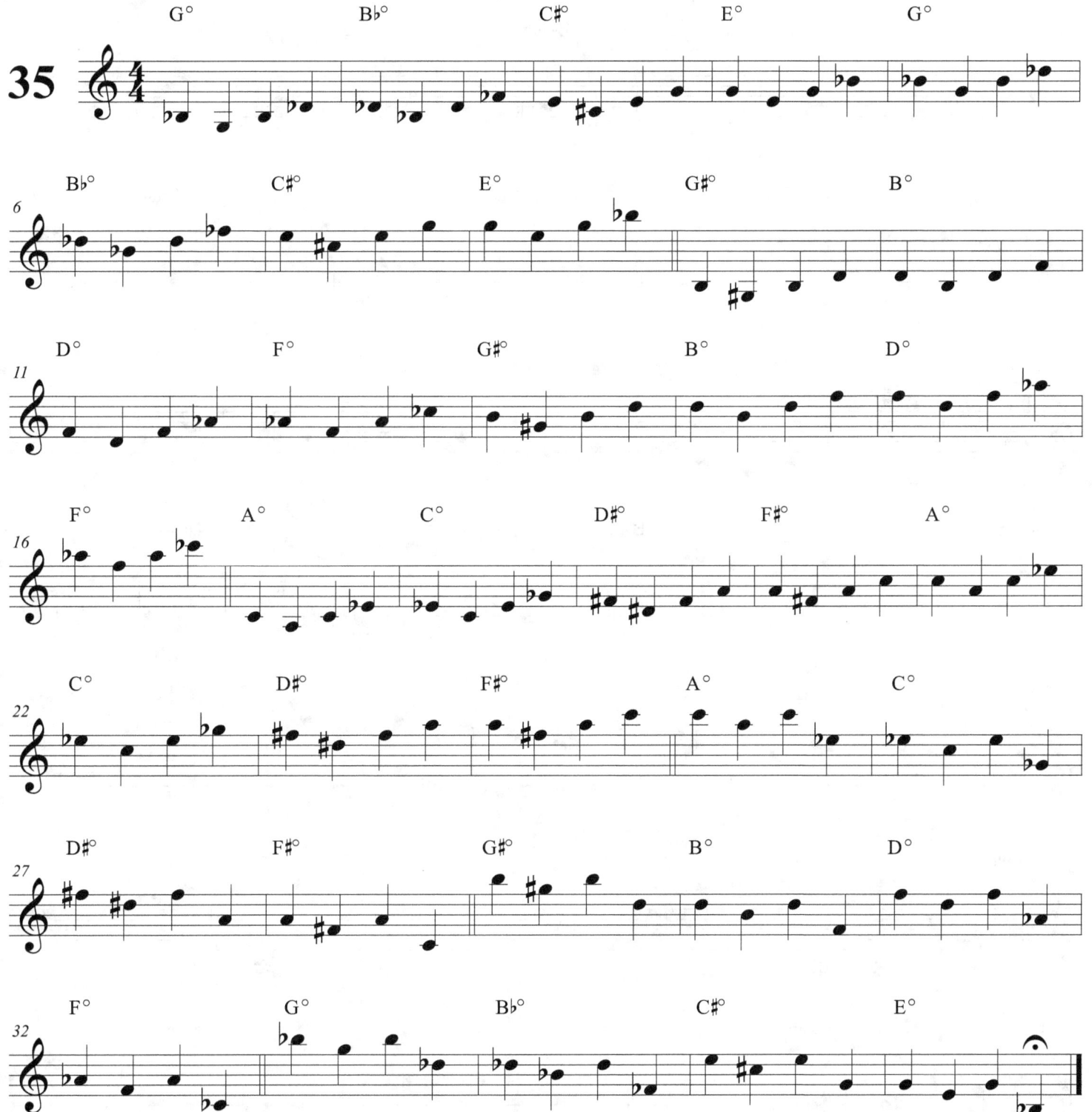

Etude 3-1-3-5
Augmented

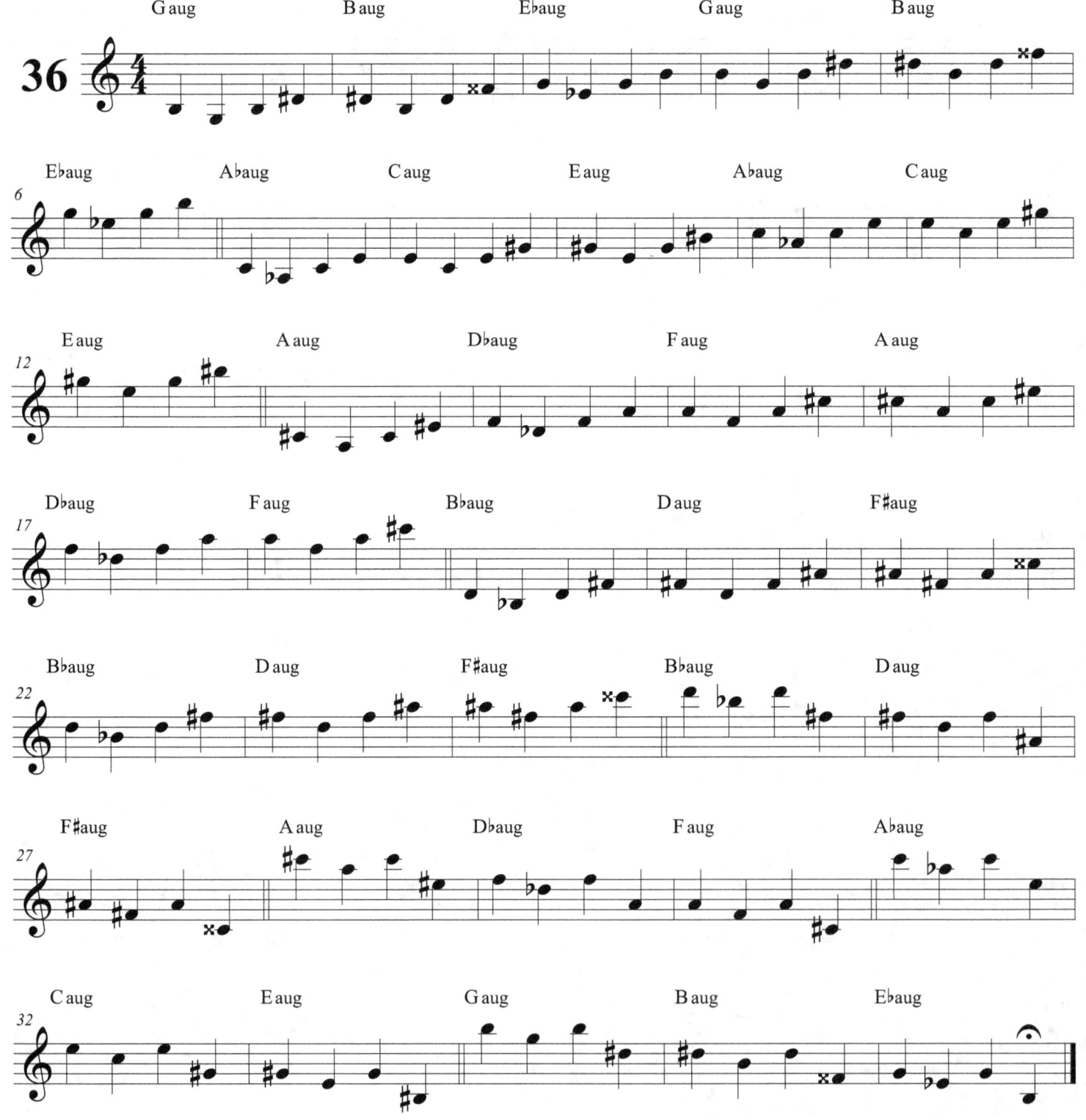

Etude 3-5-3-1
Major

37

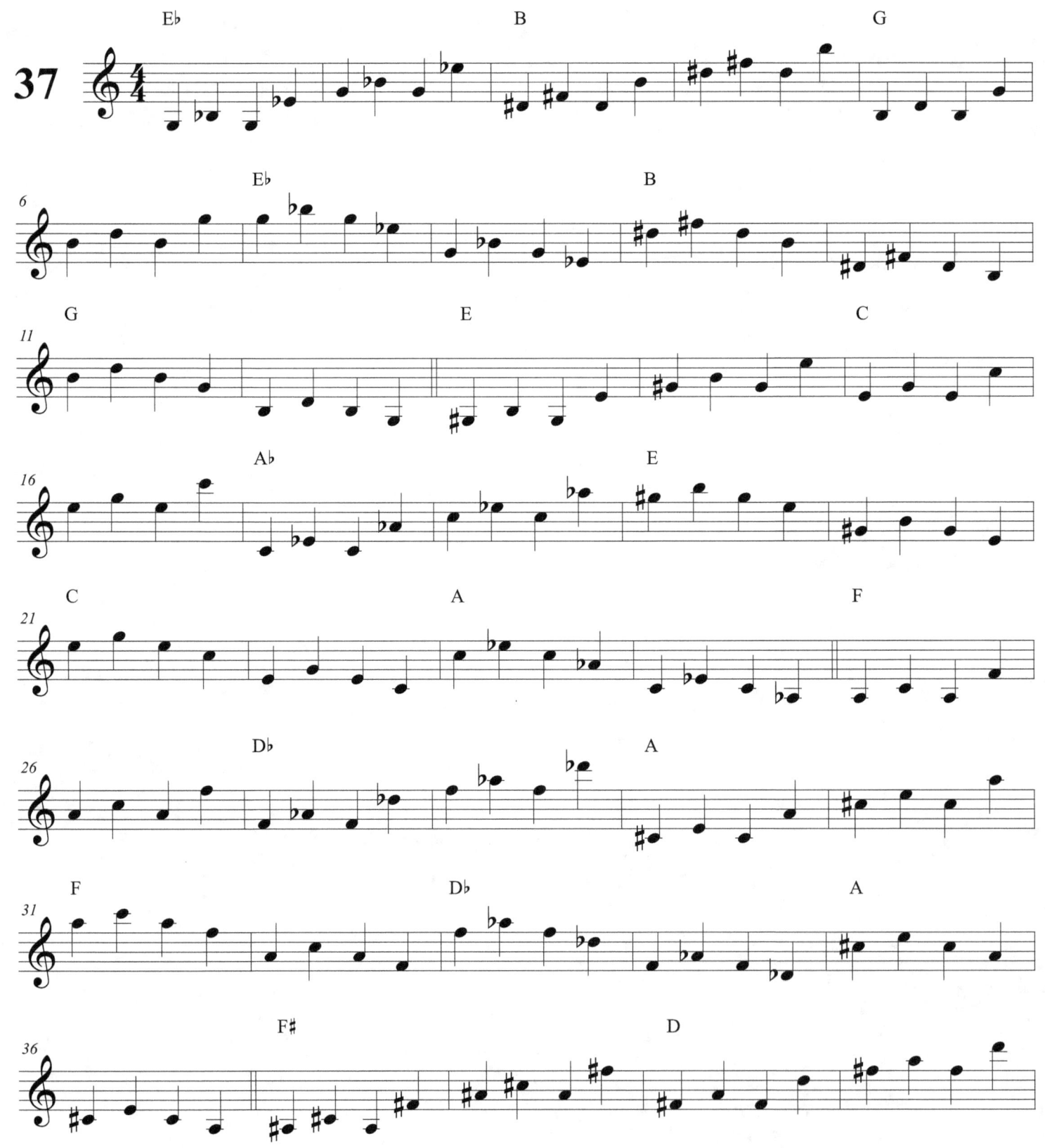

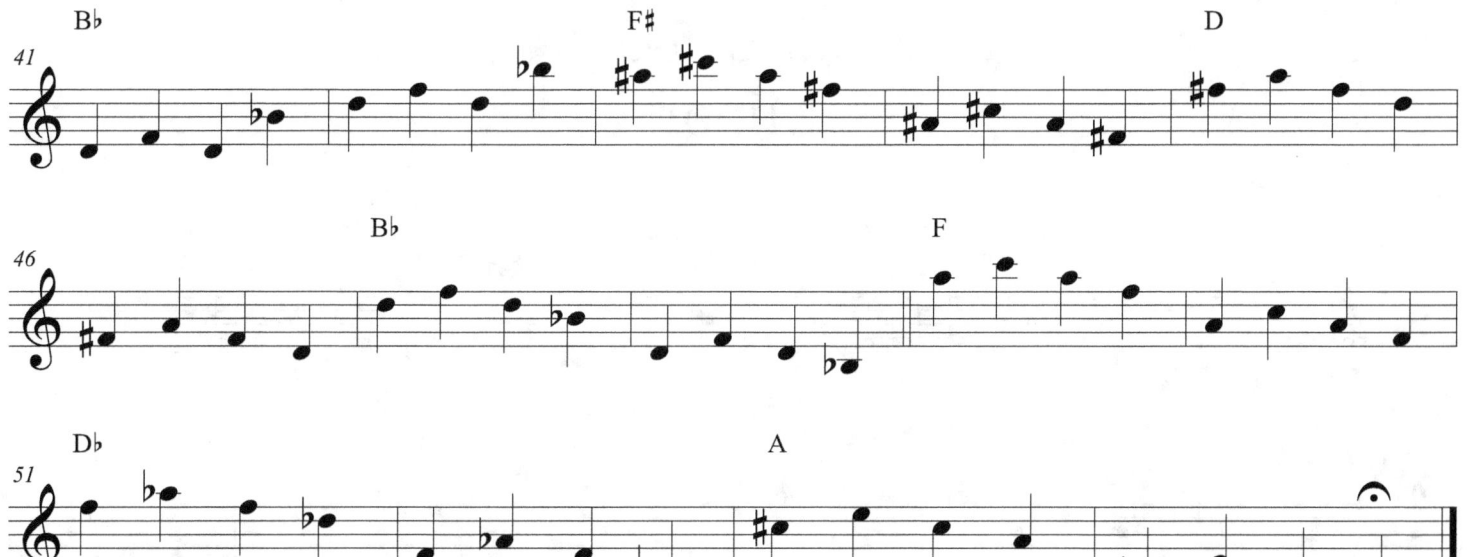

Etude 3-5-3-1
Minor

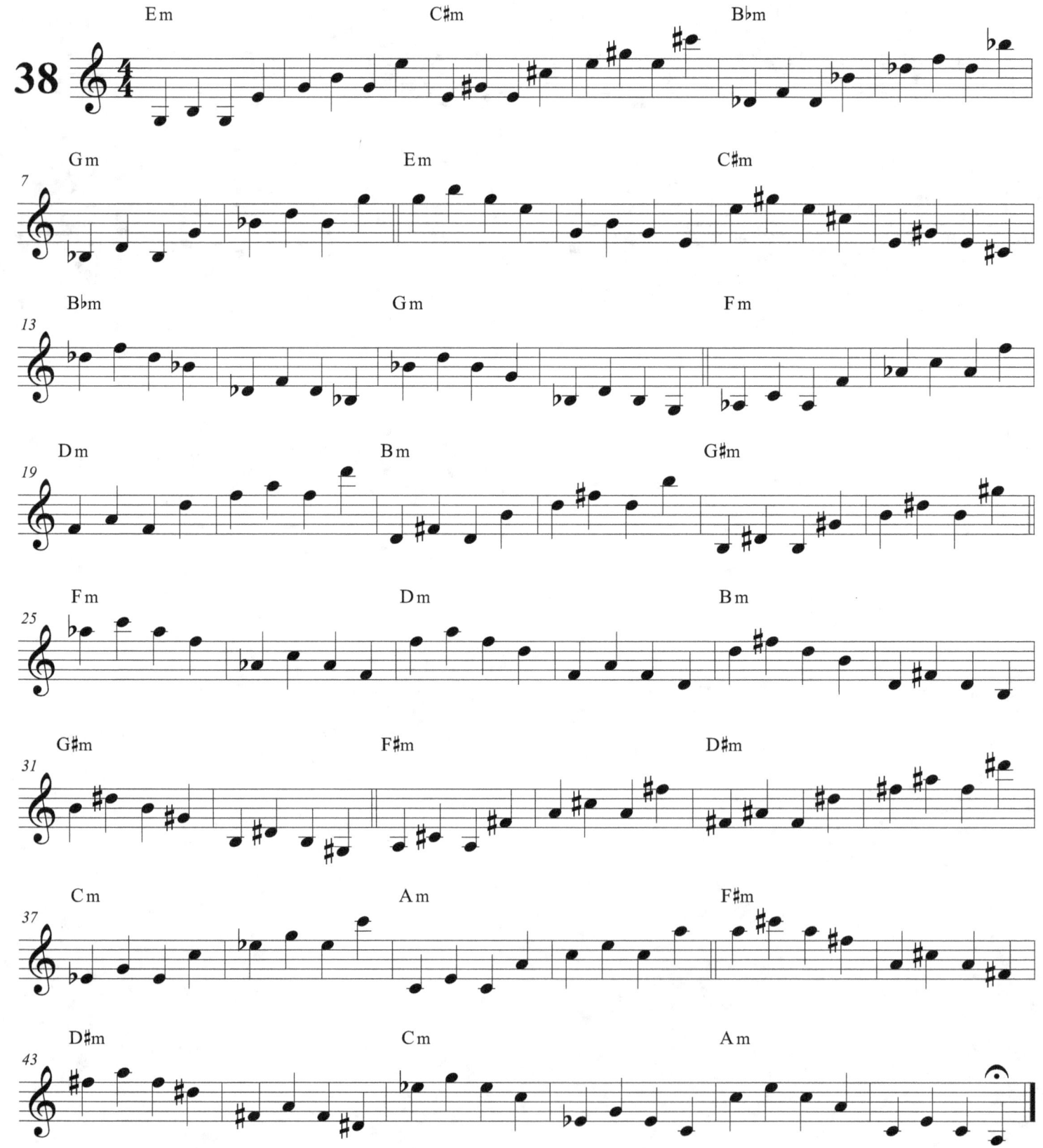

Etude 3-5-3-1
Diminished

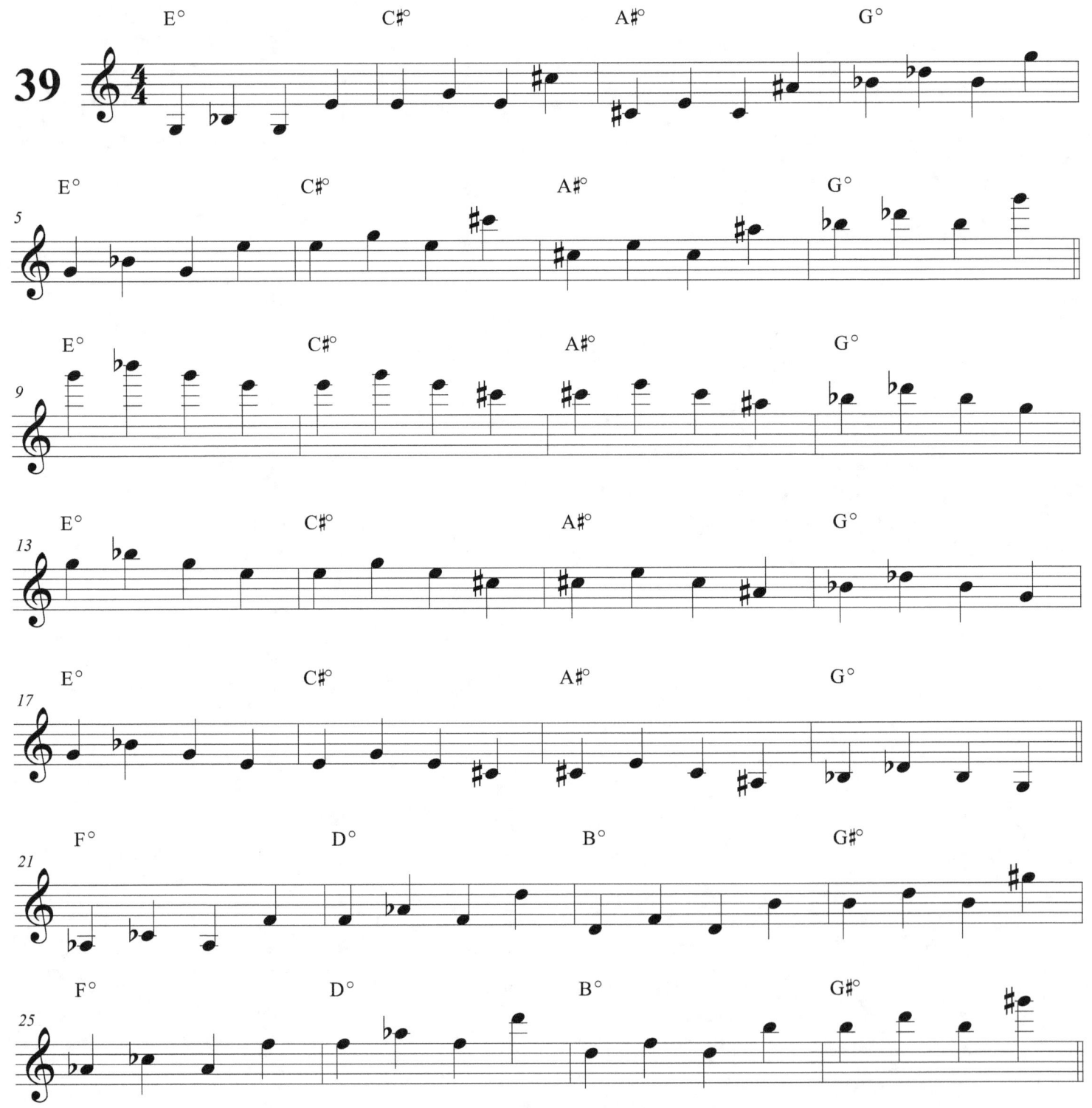

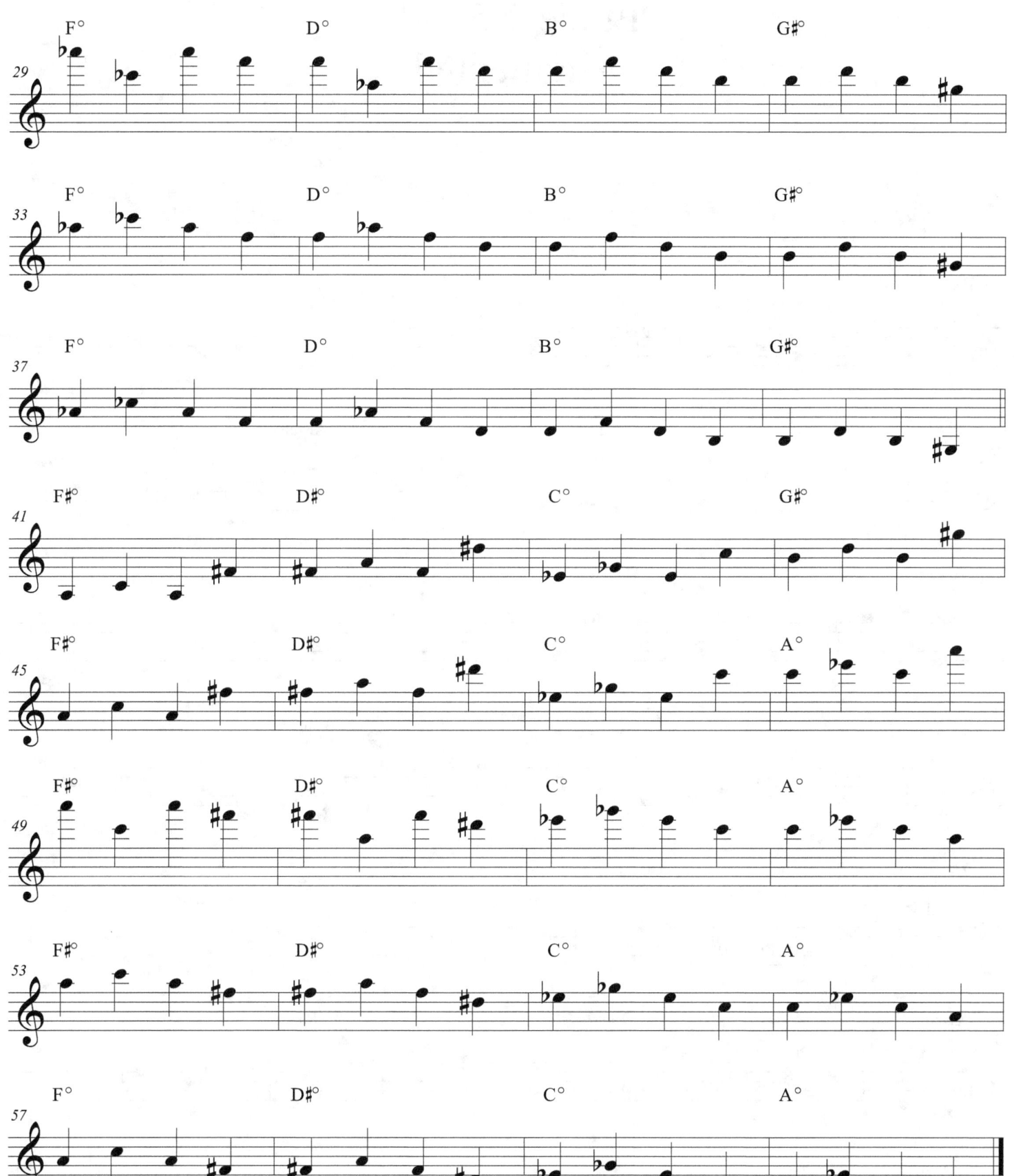

Etude 3-5-3-1
Augmented

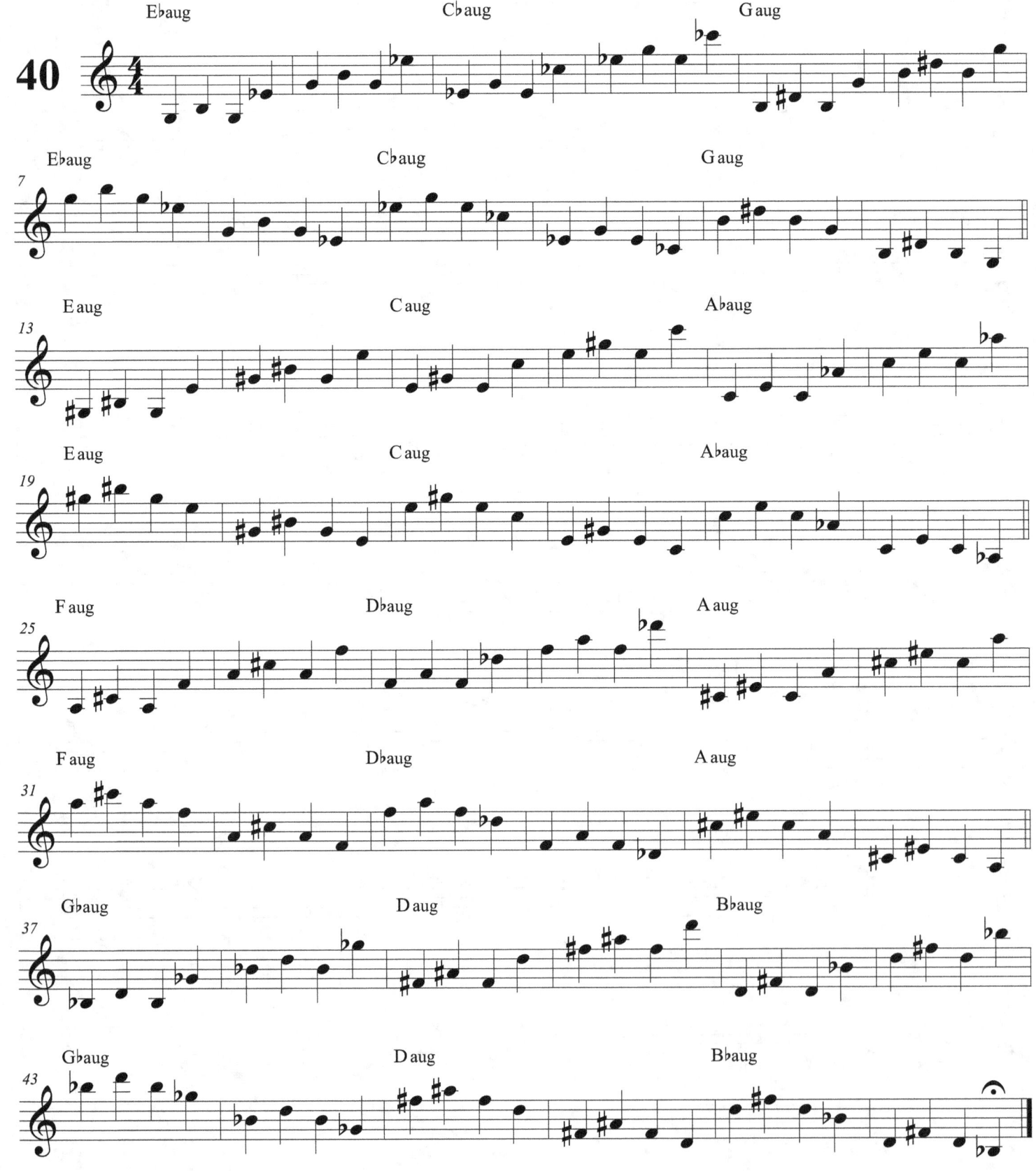

Etude 5-1-5-3
Major

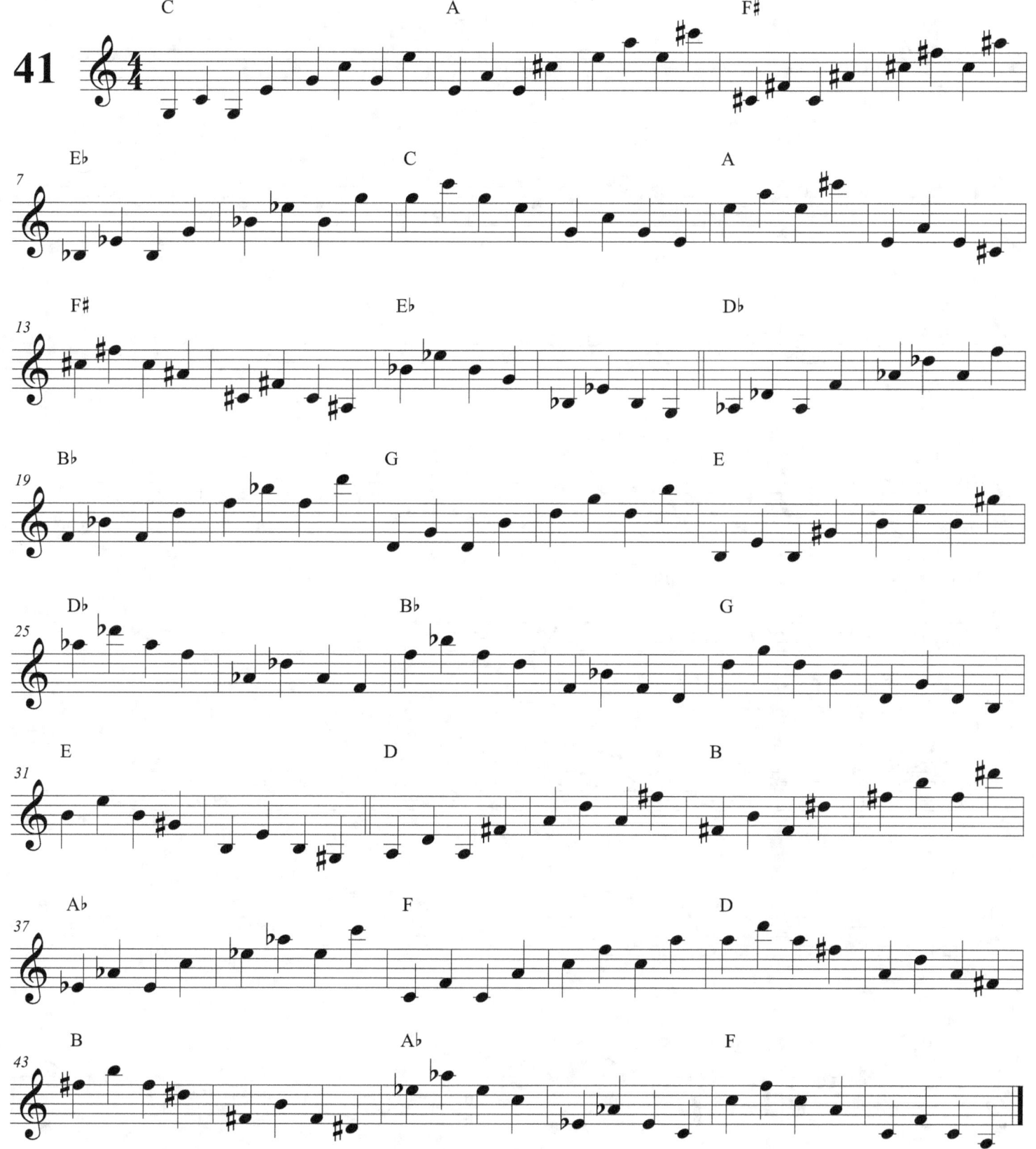

Etude 5-1-5-3
Minor

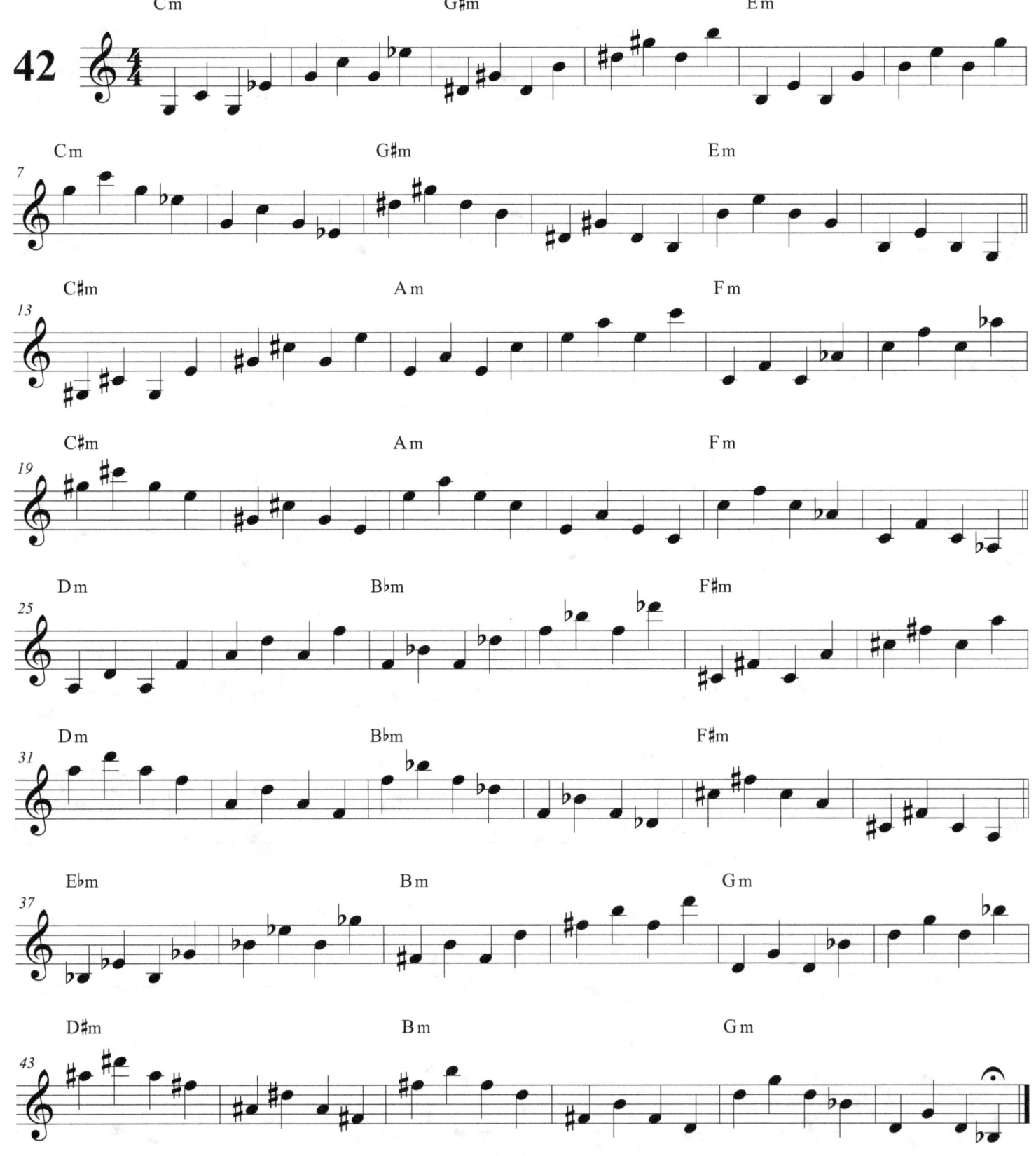

Etude 5-1-5-3
Diminished

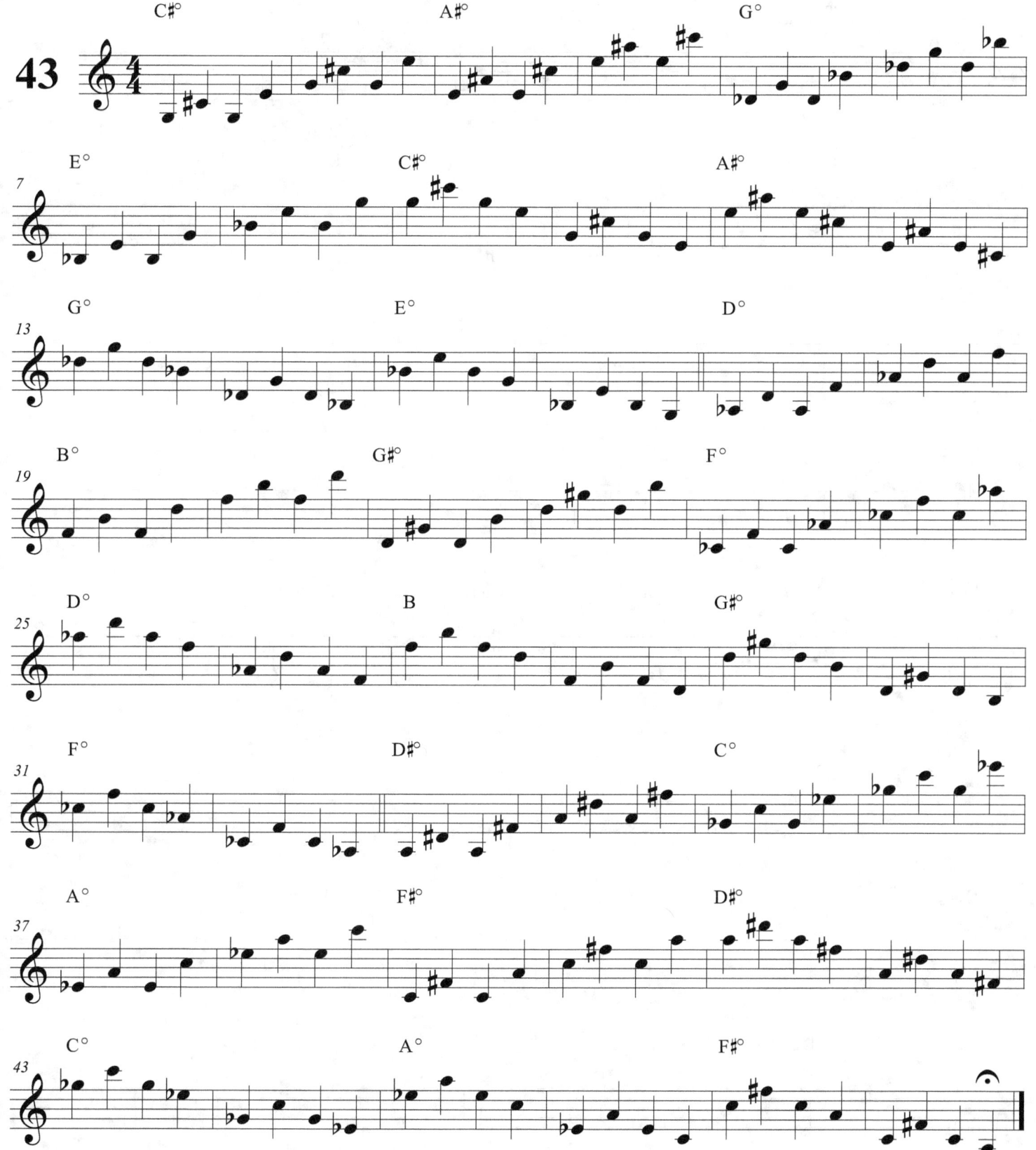

Etude 5-1-5-3
Augmented

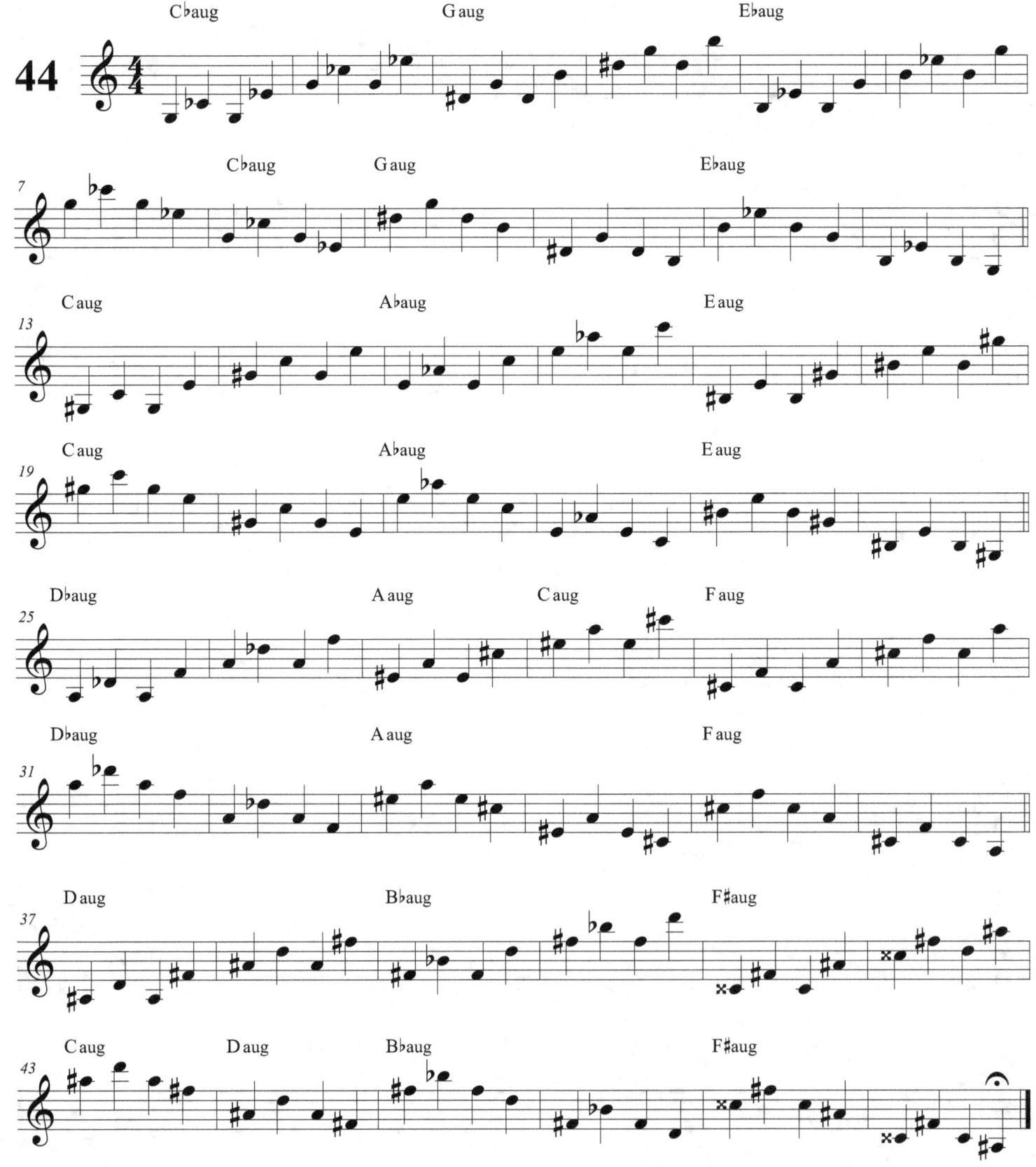

Etude 5-3-5-1
Major

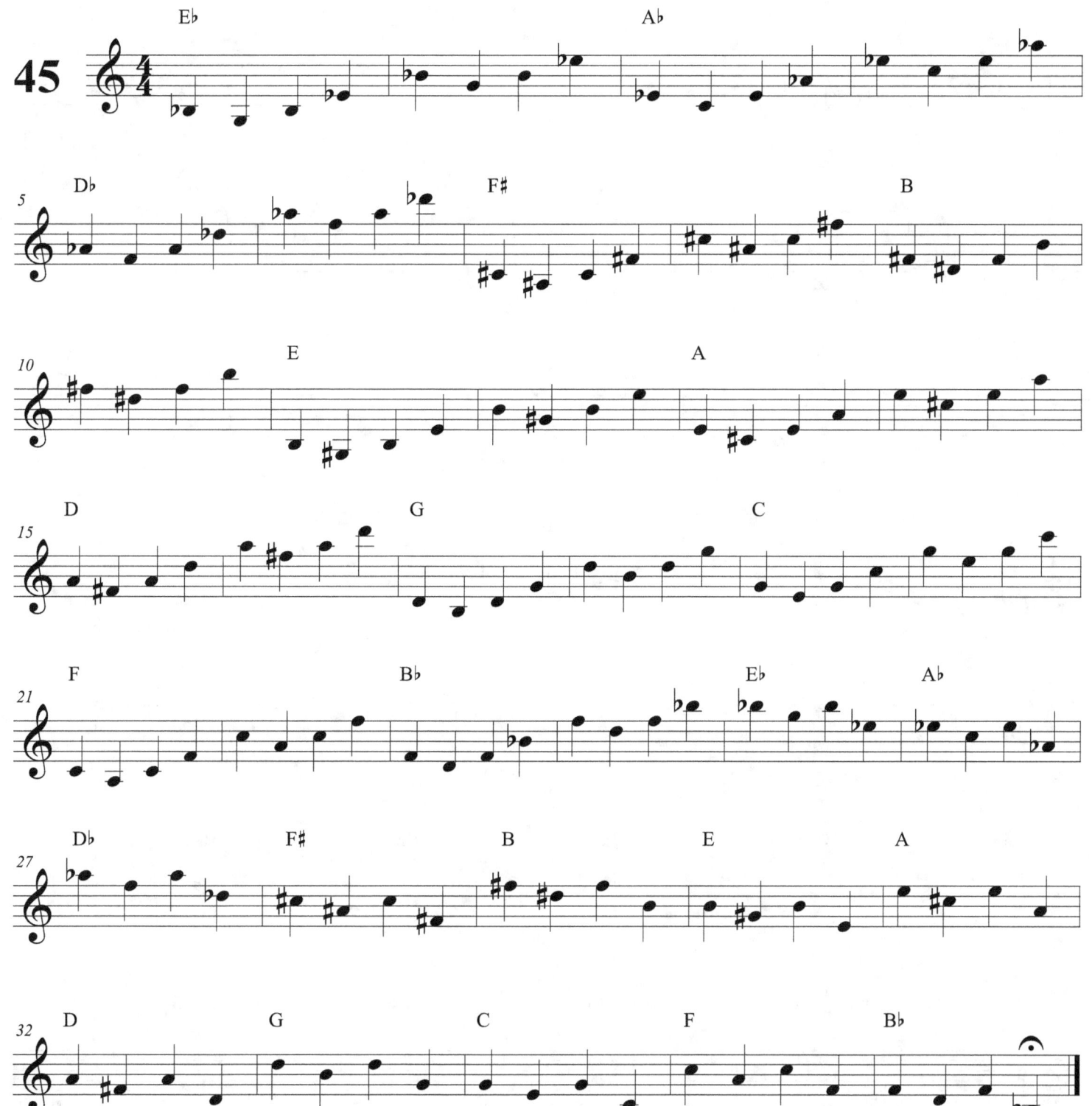

Etude 5-3-5-1
Minor

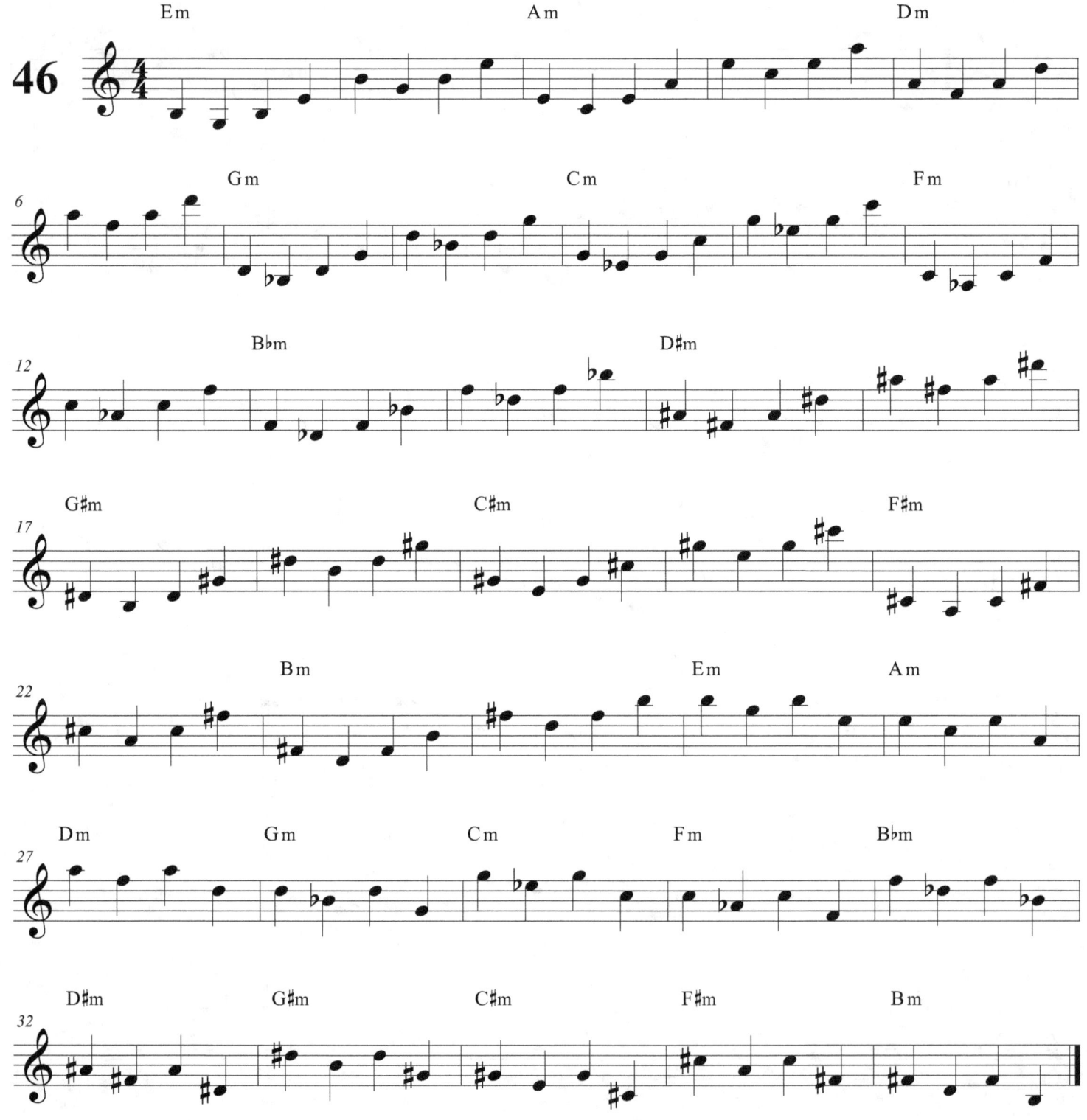

Etude 5-3-5-1
Diminished

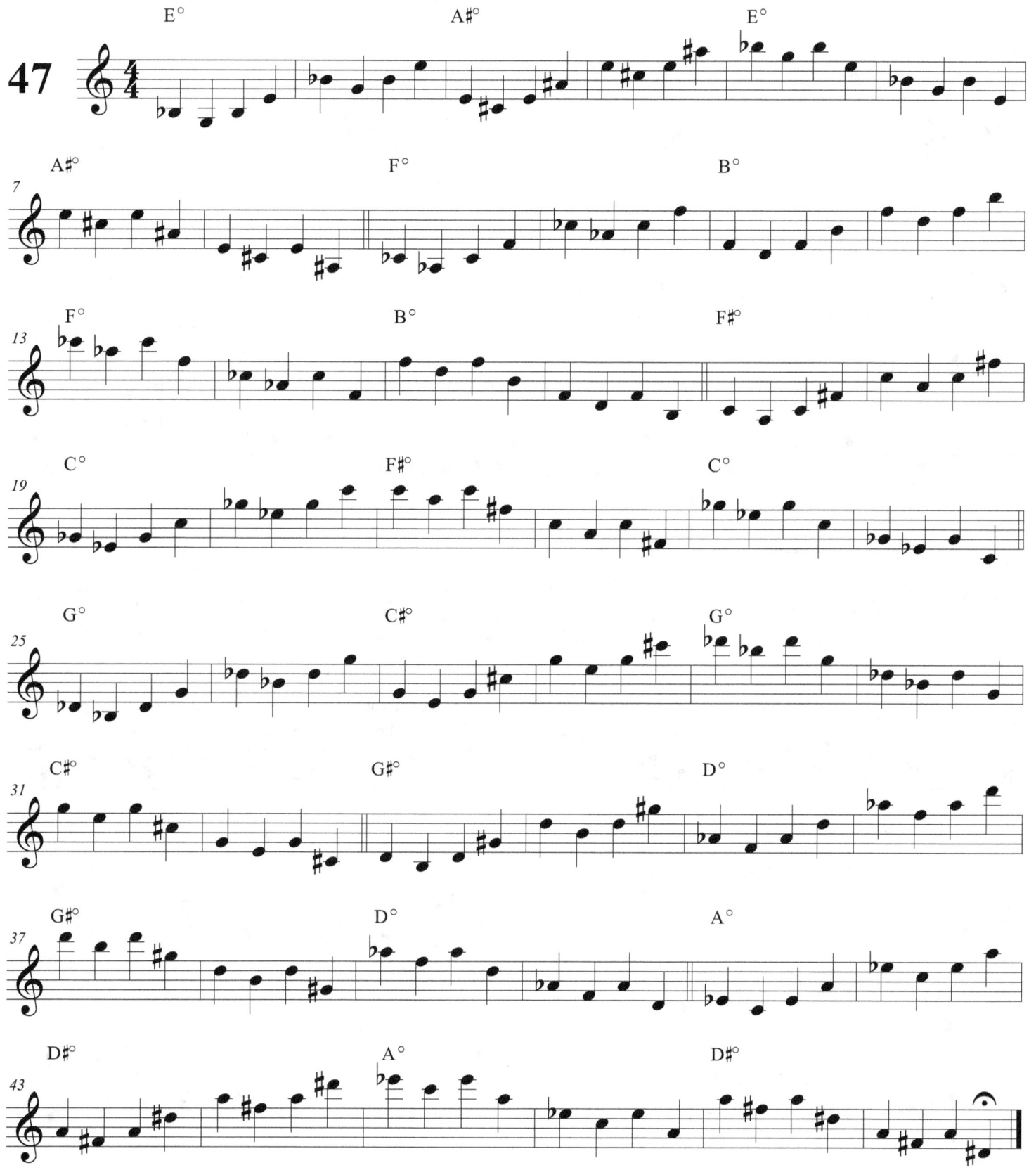

Etude 5-3-5-1
Augmented

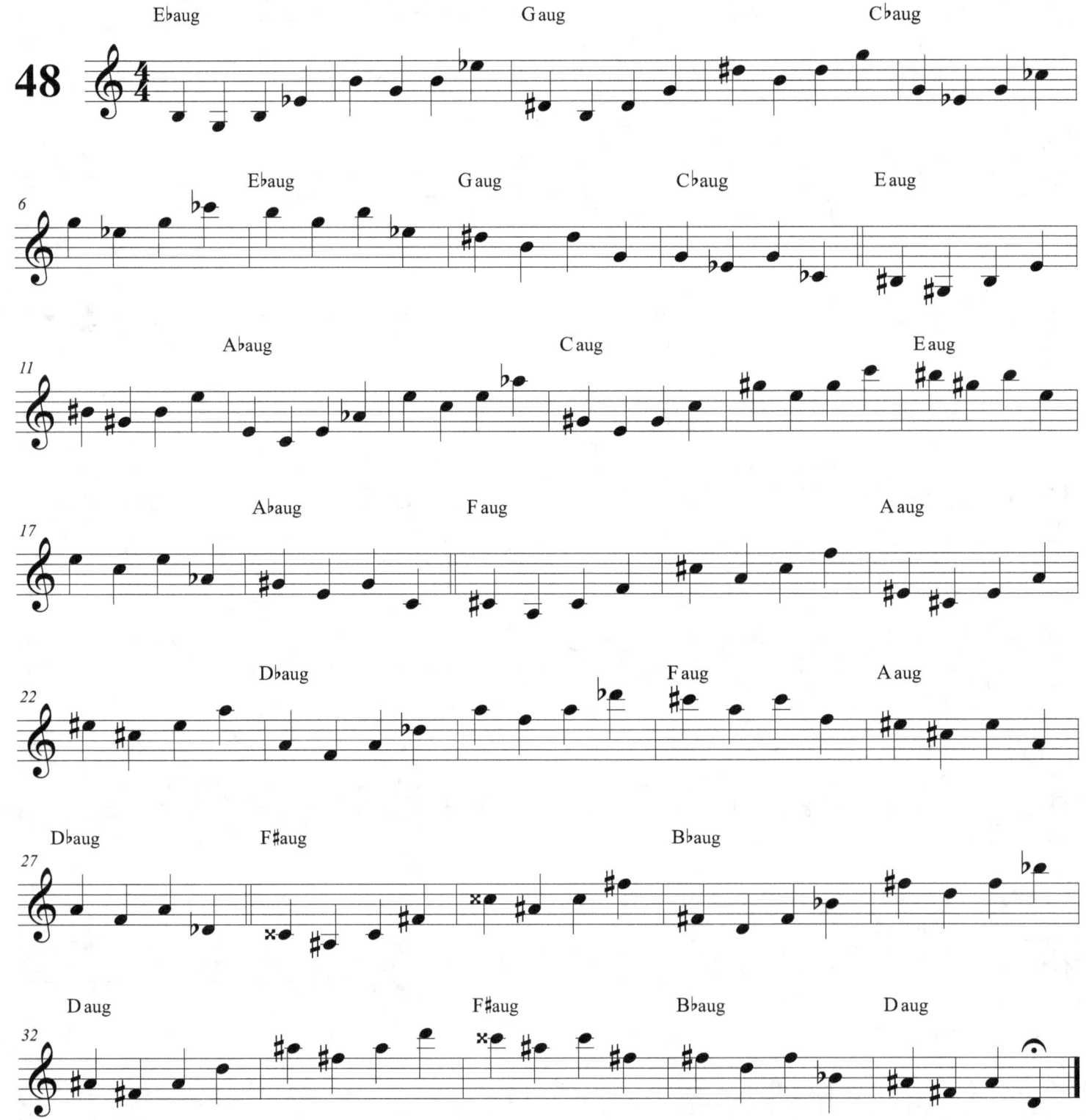

www.ingramcontent.com/pod-product-compliance
Lightning Source LLC
Chambersburg PA
CBHW081748220526
45468CB00008B/2289

If this method was to your liking and you would like to get the workbook and the 48 Mp3's totally free, please leave a positive review on Amazon, take a screenshot and send it to the email below. Within a few days you will receive it in your mail.

Si este método fue de su agrado y le gustaría obtener el cuaderno de trabajo y los 48 Mp3 totalmente gratis, por favor deje una crítica positiva en Amazon, tome una captura de pantalla y mándela al correo de más abajo. En pocos días los recibirá en su correo.

cristianromerovargas@gmail.com

Bogotá 2018